QUILTING
with Doilies

Inspiration | Techniques | Projects

BARBARA POLSTON

Schiffer Publishing Ltd
4880 Lower Valley Road • Atglen, PA 19310

Dedication

For the women in my family, who gave me a love of fine needlework in all of its forms, and for my daughters, Tracy Sagalow and Caitlyn Polston, who believe that dreams can be achieved.

Acknowledgments

Thank you to Terri Doyle, for both her beautiful quilting and photographs; Judy Taylor, for her creative quilting; Brian Boehm, idesign Graphics, for lending his graphic design expertise where needed; and Leslie Lindquist, for dotting my i's and crossing my t's. Your contributions are appreciated and invaluable.

Library of Congress Control Number: 2014954917

Cover design by Ro
Type set in Helvetica

ISBN: 978-0-7643-4699-6
Printed in China

Published by Schiffer Publishing, Ltd.
4880 Lower Valley Road
Atglen, PA 19310
Phone: (610) 593-1777; Fax: (610) 593-2002
E-mail: Info@schifferbooks.com

For our complete selection of fine books on this and related subjects, please visit our website at www.schifferbooks.com. You may also write for a free catalog.

This book may be purchased from the publisher. Please try your bookstore first.

We are always looking for people to write books on new and related subjects. If you have an idea for a book, please contact us at proposals@ schifferbooks.com.

Schiffer Publishing's titles are available at special discounts for bulk purchases for sales promotions or premiums. Special editions, including personalized covers, corporate imprints, and excerpts can be created in large quantities for special needs. For more information, contact the publisher.

Contents

Section One: The Techniques

Section Two: The Patterns

Foreword

It was once said that talent and passion can triumph over adversity on any given day. Barbara and I met while serving on a board of directors; those times and that experience was not at all what I had imagined. However, Barbara and I found common ground: October birth dates; a love of teaching; respect for strong, talented women; and a passion for quilting.

I know Barbara as a writer who produces unbelievable quilts; I'm a quilter who has something to say, so I write. We've talked about our dreams of making contemporary quilts, yet our heartstrings are pulled to the past. Countless linens have been abandoned in thrift shops, yard sales, and antique malls. They wait for a new purpose in our modern world. Barbara knows that and chooses not to leave the foundation from which we draw inspiration behind.

Barbara, a researcher, dissects like a skilled surgeon. She is a perfectionist. Over the years, she has talked about her collection of vintage linens and shared a glimpse of what "needlework" meant in the lean and painful years — and then her art exploded, winning ribbon after ribbon...art quilts. This book is a celebration of her passion for mixing the old with the new and her voice as a writer.

I can't wait to see all her creations. As an artist, she has incorporated vestiges of long-forgotten needlecrafts and repurposed them into the heart and soul of her quilts. Barbara, a renaissance woman, is challenging us to blend the edges of tradition with the spirit of the modern world.

We have come full circle in living and sharing our dream. I'm excited to see this — her first book — come to life.

—Gyleen Fitzgerald
Colourful Stitches
Havre de Grace, Maryland

Preface

Out of the Attic, 30" x 30"

I come from a long line of needlewomen. I never knew my paternal grandmother, but I do know that, as a young widow, she supported her family as a dressmaker. She made utilitarian scrap quilts, one of which Dad used to lay upon while changing the oil in the family car (much to his daughter's chagrin years later). On Mom's side, all the ladies were accomplished needlewomen who taught me my stitches and a deep respect for handwork.

I learned to embroider at age seven or eight. Mom taught me to sew on the sewing machine the summer I was nine. I remember my grandmother teaching me how to cast on in an attempt to make a knitter out of me... that distinction fell to my Aunt Lydia, who was the most excellent knitter I have ever known. Along the way, I learned to crochet and do macramé, hairpin lace, needlepoint, and counted cross stitch. In the late 1990s, I found quilting, which feels like home.

Incorporating doilies into my quilts began in 2007. I had just become the keeper of the family's crocheted and embroidered doilies, many made in the 1920s–1940s era. One particular doily spoke to me, so I asked Mom if she knew the story of its making. She did — she made it in 1941. Variegated crochet cotton had just been introduced to the market. Her then-boyfriend liked the variegated thread and challenged her to make something with it; this doily was the result.

The doily was placed in Mom's hope chest in Grandmother's attic. World War II intervened, Mom's boyfriend married another, and the doily was forgotten. It moved from Grandma's attic to Aunt Lydia's closet when she sold the family home. When she developed Alzheimer's disease, we closed down her house and moved her to an assisted living facility. All of the family needlework passed to me for safekeeping.

With a guild quilt show theme of "Out of the Attic – Old and New," I thought it would be lovely to incorporate the doily into a quilt. With Mom's permission, I created a traditional Log Cabin setting and showcased the doily in the center. This quilt hung over my fireplace for many years; I remain very fond of it, thinking of it as a lovely combination of the old and the new. I believe the doily is pleased with its new life.

Fast-forward to 2010. I had the opportunity to go to the International Quilting Association's annual show in Houston, Texas. Shopping the vendors was an amazing experience and I visited almost every booth. In one, I found a lovely, round, white linen piece with a beautiful tatted design at the edge. As soon as I touched that vintage linen, the quilt design for *Vintage Roses*, which

Happy 25th Anniversary, 34-1/4" x 34-1/2"

you will see in this book, leapt into my head — that linen piece came home with me. Although it took two years to execute, the finished quilt is very close to what I envisioned while standing in that vendor's booth.

In 2012, the Hoffman Challenge was celebrating its 25th Anniversary. The challenge fabric was done in beautiful shades of purple, my favorite color. The Silver Anniversary had me thinking of weddings, the passage of time, and how to honor this significant anniversary. Once again, I turned to vintage linen to help me execute my concept. In *Happy 25th Anniversary*, a vase of flowers sits on a table, flanked by an anniversary greeting card and a framed wedding photo from Paul and Mickey Depre's late 1980s wedding. The vase sits upon a vintage doily from my family's collection; made by my grandmother, this doily is embroidered with a crochet edge. We believe it must have been made in the 1920s and was clearly used and laundered many times. The doily adds the perfect touch to the composition.

I doubt that we'll be displaying knickknacks on doilies, resting our lamps upon them, or pinning them to the armrests and backs of our easy chairs. Decorating styles and tastes have changed. My guess is that many of us have boxes stored in closets, attics, garages, and dresser drawers. We can't bear to part with them because they are part of our family history, so, I say, let's incorporate these lovelies into contemporary quilts!

In addition to my family linens, I've amassed quite a collection of doilies found on eBay™, etsy.com, quilt show vendor malls, and antique shops. I see them and they whisper to me. They ask to be incorporated into my work; they want to be enjoyed and be useful again. Doilies inspire my quilts.

While it's impossible for you to find exactly the same linen pieces that I've used for these projects, there are many available to you from various sources. In these pages, you'll discover what each doily whispered to me — my inspiration — and we'll explore various techniques meant to expand your quilter's toolkit. Finally, several patterns for projects using vintage doilies are shared. I hope you'll use this book as a guide as you allow vintage doilies to whisper to you.

Introduction

A wide variety of vintage doilies are probably in your collection. It will be helpful to review the various types of doilies and offer suggestions for designing and working with each. We'll conclude the discussion with shopping and care tips.

These thoughts are based upon my personal experience and are not meant to be the definitive class on vintage linens. If you believe your item may have high value as a collectible or museum-quality piece, please consult with an appraiser of vintage textiles to be sure before manipulating it into your quilt. If you choose to use it, then you fully understand the choice you are making. Most vintage doilies are sold for less than $30; many more go for much less than that. To me, those costs seem reasonable for inclusion in quilts.

Types of Vintage Doilies

Crochet Doilies

In general, these doilies were made with fine cotton thread, manipulated into their patterns by working the thread with a single crochet hook. Most were made by beginning with a central ring and working rounds of stitches. Larger pieces were created by either adding additional rounds or by working with thicker thread and a larger hook. The finer the thread and the smaller the hook used, the tighter and smaller the stitches. When these items are washed or cleaned, they lose their shape and become messy looking. Our grandmothers starched and blocked them each time they were laundered.

Examples of crochet doilies.

Positives

These pieces generally offer an "airy" look. Finer-stitched pieces have a delicate appearance. These doilies can certainly add to the particular tone of a quilt.

Considerations

There are several, including:

- These pieces were originally worked with one long thread. If you plan to cut the piece, you run the risk of the thread unraveling. With finer crochet work — thinner thread, smaller hook, and tighter stitches — this risk is diminished. Because the thread has spent so many years locked into its shape, it has a desire to stay where it is. However, the risk should be considered before cutting the crochet work.
- Your design will require a background fabric under the crochet work.
- If you first clean your vintage crochet doily — and I recommend that — you will need to block it back into shape. See the blocking tutorial at the end of the cleaning section.
- It is a challenge to attach crochet doilies to your quilt top by machine. After trying several different methods, my best recommendation is to hand-stitch the crocheted piece to the fabric. Pin well and stitch from the center

out in concentric rounds with thread that matches the color of the doily. Heavier stitching will ensure the doily will keep its shape if the quilt is ever subjected to water.

- For the same reasons, it's challenging to quilt over the top of crocheted doilies. Free-motion lines of quilting where crocheted rounds join work well. Use your hopping foot, which floats above the surface of the doily, and slow your speed in case the foot catches in the crochet work, so that you can stop and free it. Again, the quilting lines will help the doily keep its shape if the quilt ever becomes wet, whether that's intentional or not.

Fabric Centers With or Without Embroidery

In these vintage doilies, fabric centers may be embellished with embroidery and there may, or may not, be a crocheted or tatted edging worked around the doily. If there's no crochet or tatting, there's usually a tight, machine-worked satin stitch to finish off the edging, or they are finished with a buttonhole stitch. Generally, the central fabric piece is a looser weave to help the hand-stitcher work the needle through the fabric to create her embroidery designs. If the fabric is a tighter weave, you can bet that the thread embellishments were executed in a manufacturing environment, although there's nothing wrong with that.

Examples of fabric center doilies with (left) and without (right) embroidery.

Positives

These doilies provide a wide variety of appearances and applications to quilt projects. It's possible to cut background fabric away from behind the solid linen sections so there's no shadowing through of background fabric. These linen pieces can be a good base for appliqué.

Considerations

- If the base fabric is linen, rather than a cotton or cotton blend, it has a tendency to wrinkle as it is manipulated. Planning for dense quilting over the linen ensures a wrinkle-free final appearance.
- You may need to hand-stitch down the crochet or tatted edge finishes.
- If your piece has embroidery, plan for how you will showcase that feature.

Chemical Lace Doilies

These doilies are manufactured — and the process is fascinating. A tightly-woven fabric center is placed upon a background and then intricate designs are stitched, catching the edge of the center fabric and creating a lace edge. The piece is then plunged into a chemical bath and the background fabric dissolves away, leaving the lace and center cloth behind. The lace often has cherubs and ornate urns worked into the detailed designs. These features set a particular tone for the finished project.

An example of a doily with a chemical lace outer edge.

Positives

These doilies are just downright impressive! Background fabric can be cut away from behind the center fabric so there's no shadowing through of background fabric. They make a good base for appliqué and placement of words.

Considerations

- It's easy to break the bar stitches that join the larger lace elements together. Treat these linen pieces delicately.
- Attaching the delicate lace to your base fabric can be a challenge. I believe the best method is to turn the linen into a fusible appliqué piece using SpraynBond™ fusible adhesive by Therm-O-Web, Inc. With this method, you will not be able to remove base fabric from behind, however.

Cutwork or Madeira Doilies

I often find cutwork doilies identified as Madeira embroidery after the technique developed in Madeira, Portugal, as a cottage industry in the late 1860s. Fine satin stitches are worked in patterns over tightly-woven base fabric, which is cut away to create open elements within the design. There are many white-on-white pieces available, but it's also possible to find pieces worked in colored threads. Beautiful!

Examples of cutwork doilies.

Positives

The tightly-woven base fabric supports appliqué, painted, or embroidered designs well. Unusually shaped work, such as flowers, increase design possibilities. A wide variety of shapes and sizes make these a flexible design element for quilts. They are also easy to attach to background fabric by machine.

Considerations

- Requires a background fabric due to the open areas of the doily design. While dark fabric behind can be dramatic, the dark color will shadow through the doily.
- Consider dense quilting patterns over the doily to prevent wrinkling of the doily's base fabric.

Sheer Fabric Doilies

These charming doilies are made of sheer fabric with designs created by building layered bits of fabrics or threads.

Positives

The sheer base fabric adds a bit of sheen to the project and mutes the background fabric, increasing design possibilities. Easy to machine stitch to background fabric.

Considerations

- Requires a background fabric base.
- Does not support appliqué or painted elements well.

Examples of sheer fabric doilies.

Battenburg Lace Doilies

Easily identifiable, this work is referred to by many names, including Renaissance lace, tape lace, and mezzo punto. It's worked by manipulating even-width, woven tapes into a variety of shapes with stitches (called bars or brides) holding the designs together and filling in gaps. Doilies may be made entirely of this technique or the tape lace may be used as edging. This style of lace-making was developed in Victorian England and every English duke had his own lace pattern. The making of this lace is less labor intensive and contemporary pieces are readily available.

Doilies crafted completely of (left) or edged in (right) Battenburg lace.

Positives

Generally, sturdily made and easy to machine stitch to fabric surfaces.

Considerations

- Tape lace will tighten and pucker when it becomes wet. Quilting needs to be planned to hold the shape of the doily if the quilt will be laundered.
- Using these doilies will require the use of a background fabric.

Shopping for Vintage Doilies

If you don't have a collection of vintage doilies already, they are easy to find. You don't need to be an expert on vintage linens to make purchases that will suit your needs and tastes. Set a budget and stick to it! If you decide you don't want to spend more than $10 for a doily, then don't. Allow the doily to whisper to you — and you will soon discover the perfect find!

eBay (www.ebay.com)

eBay offers a couple of nice options. In the search box, enter "vintage embroidered doily," "vintage lace doily," or "vintage crochet doily." You can search just by that term or narrow your search by entering "before 1930s" or "1930s to now." A recent search for embroidered doilies brought over 650 selections to scroll through. When you see something that catches your eye, click on the listing.

Once on the listing, read the seller's description of the item. Pay special attention to measurements. If you have a hard time visualizing size, get your ruler or tape measure out to give yourself a better visual. Pay particular attention to any disclosures on tears or stains. Take full advantage of the ability to enlarge the item photos and scroll around them to see the item in the most detail possible. I particularly look for fraying about the edges and the quality of the embroidery stitches, if that's part of the doily's design.

Take note of where the doily will be shipped from and the shipping costs that will be added on top of the selling price. Some sellers allow you to "Buy it Now." I like this feature, because if I want the piece I can complete the transaction and it's in my mailbox within a few days. Note that eBay purchases are auction only, so if you love it, set your top price and bid. It's exciting and fun when you win!

Etsy (www.etsy.com)

Etsy is one of my favorite places to shop. It's an on-line marketplace of every possible handmade item. The descriptions on etsy are a bit more precise. A search of "doily in vintage" brought up over 16,500 items to view, but included vintage paper doilies and other assorted items. A search of "embroidered doily in vintage" returned almost 1,900 items and "crocheted doily in vintage" almost 9,500 items. You may sort your results by price or "most recently added" to the site. Find something that appeals to you and click on the listing.

Once there, read the seller's description of the item and follow the advice given above. Most sellers have a zoom feature on their item photos. Take full advantage of that to look at the detail of the doily.

Take note of where the doily is shipping from and the shipping costs that will be added on top of the selling price. On etsy, there's no bidding, so if you like the item and find the price and shipping costs acceptable, you can buy it with a few clicks of your mouse. If you buy several different items from several different sellers, you will need to complete a different purchase transaction for each seller — and then start watching your mail for the arrival of your purchases!

Antique Shops and Malls

I have found baskets of vintage doilies in antique shops. Some are used as parts of displays, showcasing knickknacks atop antique dressers. If it is in the shop, it's probably for sale! The search through a basket can be fun or overwhelming. Approach this in a way that feels right for you. You might carefully go through each piece or quickly dig through the basket, hoping something will catch your eye.

The nice thing about shopping for your treasures in person is that you can inspect the item fully, something online sites don't offer. In-person shopping means the opportunity to see the back of the work. Especially with embroidered work, I prefer that threads be finished off neatly and not travel extensive distances from one place to another. Those traveling threads will often shadow through on the front of the work and detract from the finished piece. However, that's my personal preference. If it doesn't bother you, then by all means — rescue that treasure!

I have found, on occasion, some room for price negotiation in antique shops and malls. If you would like a price reduction on a piece, don't hesitate to ask. If the answer is negative, no harm done. However, if it's yes, you will feel so much better about your find.

Thrift Stores and Resale Shops

Thrift stores and resale shops often have vintage doilies available, especially in thrift stores run by nonprofit organizations that accept any donated items for resale. Follow the same advice about shopping in an antique shop; however, don't expect to negotiate prices — they are already at rock bottom!

Estate Sales

Estate sales are great places to find vintage doilies and textiles of all varieties. In an estate sale situation, the family offering the goods for sale has generally engaged the services of a company that specializes in running the sale. They know the local market, understand what prices items will command, and know what is offered for sale. When I go to an estate sale, I find the person running the sale and ask if there are any vintage linens or textiles being offered. If some are available, I'm taken right to them. If not, I've saved time. Prices at estate sales are fairly reasonable. However, if you're buying a lot, don't hesitate to ask if that's the best pricing possible.

Cleaning Vintage Doilies

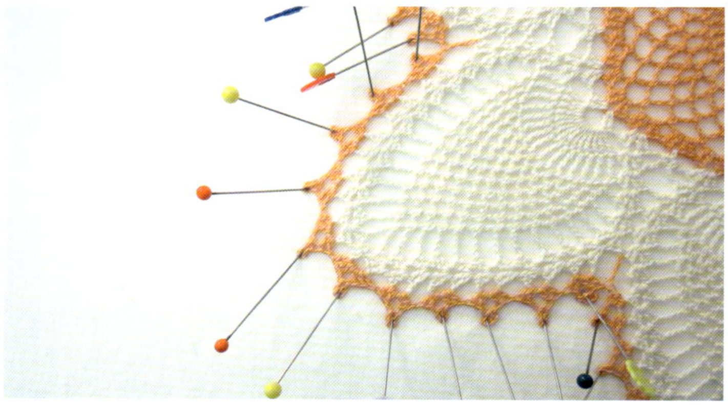

Blocking a crochet doily on flannel-covered insulation board.

If you're pulling vintage doilies out of your attic, do you remember if they were cleaned before they were stored? Has the online seller promised you that items are laundered and ready for use? Better wash those doilies before using them in your project!

There are many wonderful products available for the cleaning of vintage quilts and textiles. An online search will give you lots of different advice on products and techniques to use. If you have friends who collect vintage quilts, don't hesitate to ask how they care for their old textiles and follow their advice.

I've had great success with a product called Retro Clean. It's a gentle soaking agent designed to safely remove yellow and brown stains resulting from age. It's easy to use, just requiring a sunny, outdoor area in which to place your soaking tub. I've been very surprised that doilies I thought were pale coffee or cream colors were indeed snowy white. There's no fading or bleaching out of colors either. Retro Clean is available on the company's website, www.retroclean.com. If you need it, you can watch a video tutorial on the product's use.

Certain doilies will need to be blocked; others will not. For example, a Madeira-embroidered piece, once cleaned and dried, can be nicely finished with a good steam pressing. Crochet pieces will need blocking and a bit of starch to finish nicely.

To block a doily, you'll need a padded surface and rust-proof straight pins. A clean, folded bath towel or flannel-covered insulation board works well for the padded surface. My grandmother and mother always sprayed damp crocheted doilies with starch and then, working on the padded surface, stretched and urged the doily into shape. When the right shape was achieved, they pinned the doily down, inserting pins at a bit of an angle and creating tension on the doily. Once the doily is fully dry, remove the pins — you will have a clean, flat piece ready to use.

Section One: The Techniques

Chapter 1:

Vintage Roses & Vintage Roses Too

The design for *Vintage Roses* literally leapt into my head, fully conceptualized, when I touched the tatted linen piece that graces its central medallion. The quilt was finished with my partner, Terri Doyle. We then made *Vintage Roses Too* to showcase the techniques in its larger counterpart and as a teaching sample.

Vintage Roses, 62" x 63-1/2". Quilted by Terri Doyle.

Painted Appliqué

Do you love the look of intricate appliqué, but feel intimidated by the number of pieces needed to achieve the detail and depth? Painted Appliqué offers the same results with ONE appliqué piece.

Materials & Supplies

- Painted appliqué element: in this sample, a red rose
- Light-weight fusible interfacing (normally used for clothing construction)
- Fabric glue (Sewline™ Fabric Glue Pen or Fabric Glue Stick by Dritz® work well)
- Toothpicks or bamboo skewers
- Clear monofilament thread (poly, NOT nylon) and bobbin thread to match the color of your appliqué
- Miscellaneous: Pencil, light box or light source for pattern tracing, sharp scissors for trimming and clipping, paper towel to protect work surface, good task lighting, and your sewing machine

Rose painted on muslin. The paint is feathered beyond the outer edge for appliqué turn under.

About the Painted Element

I paint on good quality muslin that has been washed, dried (no dryer sheet), and pressed. I transfer my pattern to the muslin with a light pencil line and paint with Jacquard® Textile Colors. Following the manufacturer's instructions, the piece is heat-set once dry. It's then ready to be turned into an appliqué element.

The Method

Step 1 Using the same pattern used to paint your element, trace the exterior shape onto the non-fusible side of the interfacing, making sure to reverse the pattern. Cut the interfacing just inside the drawn line.

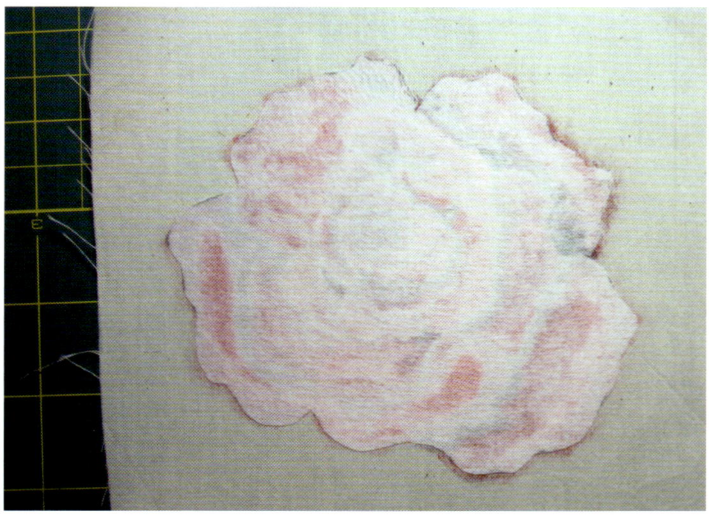

Check the fit of the fusible interfacing, trim if necessary, and fuse in place.

Step 2 Check the fit of the interfacing to the back of the painted element. You want the edge of the interfacing to lie just inside the outer edge of the painted element. Mark any areas that need trimming with a pencil and cut excess away. Following the manufacturer's instructions, fuse the interfacing to the wrong side of the painted element. Trim the muslin a scant 1/4" from the interfacing. Clip muslin every 1/4" or so around the entire piece. Make sure to clip into corners and around curves.

Clip turn under allowance and glue.

Step 3: Working around the piece, glue the turn under allowance down. It is easier to work in small sections, pushing the muslin pieces down with a toothpick or bamboo skewer.

Completed painted appliqué rose.

Step 4: Once the glue has dried, inspect your edges. If any muslin shows, use a matching colored permanent marker to fill in those places.

Machine appliqué painted elements in place.

Step 5: Pin the prepared painted appliqué piece in place on your quilt top. Thread your machine with polyester monofilament in the top and thread that matches the appliqué piece in the bottom. Use your machine's blind hem stitch, reducing the width and length of stitch, to sew to the quilt top.

Step 6: You may want to cut the fabric away from behind the appliqué piece. This will allow batting to loft into the appliqué piece and offer additional dimension.

Painted Appliqué – After Quilting

The golden scrolls in *Vintage Roses Too* were painted after quilting. Disappointed that the quilted designs weren't readily visible, we looked for the perfect product to paint already-quilted surfaces. We wanted to avoid a product that required heat-setting, as that process would compress the batting. Perfect Pigment™ by U.S. ArtQuest, Inc. seemed the perfect solution. The non-toxic, acrylic paint is permanent when dry, no heat-setting required. Metallic and pearlescent paints are also offered.

Vintage Roses Too! – Before, 40" x 40". Quilted by Terri Doyle.

Vintage Roses Too! – After

Materials & Supplies

- Quilted quilt, may be bound or not
- Small, square-tipped paint brush(es)
- Perfect Pigment™ acrylic paint by U.S. ArtQuest, Inc.
- Flat, well-lit work surface

The Method

Step 1: Finish all the quilting in your project and then select the areas you would like to accent with color. Lay the quilt on a flat, well-lit work surface.

Step 2: Using a smaller-size, square-edge brush, carefully and gently fill in the designated areas. It is not necessary to work the paint all the way to the stitching, just as close as possible. If you are right handed, work from left to right. If you are left-handed, work from right to left. This keeps your hand out of wet paint and helps eliminate unwanted paint transfer. Use care and go slowly. It will be impossible to remove unwanted paint spills or splashes from your finished quilt.

Step 3: Allow paint to dry thoroughly. If you've not yet bound and finished your quilt, do so and admire your handiwork!

Before – Terri's beautiful quilting didn't stand out.

After – Painting the quilting design elements made the quilting pop.

Double-Tabbed Edge Finish

Add this impressive finishing touch to your quilts. *Vintage Roses Too* is used as the sample project quilt for these directions.

Materials & Supplies

- Fabric for half-circles (scoops), tabs, and attaching strips. The same fabric was used for the attaching strips and scoops. The project required 1 yard. For the tabs, 1/2 yard was used.
- Light-weight fusible interfacing to back half of circle and tab fabrics
- Tape measure and protractor

The Method

This edge finish requires a bit of planning and some math. You will need a quilted top with at least a 1" margin beyond the outside quilting line. For the best finish possible, it is recommended that you block your quilt top before applying this edge finish. In the blocking, strive for square, straight edges.

Step 1: Cut excess top, batting, and backing fabric so that you have a 1" margin beyond the edge of the quilting.

Step 2: Measure each side of the quilt. Be precise. Determine the width for scoops. The goal is to have the edges of the scoops touch along the binding assembly. The second layer of tabs allows for some flexibility in this matching; some may overlap slightly and there may be a small amount of space between others. Another consideration is having an odd or even number of scoops. Scoops between 3" and 4" in diameter and an odd number are best. The odd number allows you to place a scoop in the center of each side.

For the sample project, I needed to fill a 36" edge with scoops. Wanting an odd number, I decided 11 scoops would be right. I divided 36" by 11 scoops for a result of 3.272 inches. I rounded that down to 3-1/4", which is the finished diameter of the scoop. To this measurement, add 1/2".

Step 3: Cut attaching strips. You will need strips that are 1-1/4" wide and you will use two for each side. For my project, I cut 8 strips 1-1/4" wide by width of fabric. If you need longer strips, piece them using a 45 degree angle seam and press open to reduce bulk.

Step 4: Prepare the circle pattern piece. Using a protractor, draw a circle with the diameter determined in Step 2; in our example 3-3/4". Make several paper patterns of the same size.

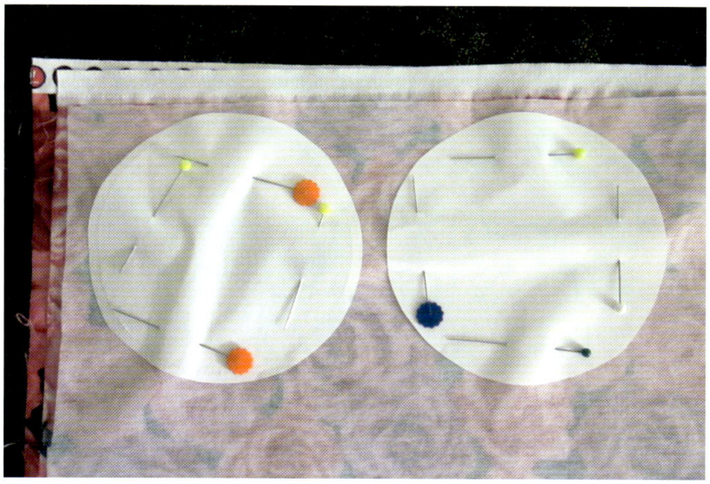

Prepare the fabric and patterns, and cut circles and scoops.

Step 5: Fuse lightweight interfacing to half of the remaining scoop fabric. You will need half as many circles as the number of scoops required. I needed 44 scoops or 22 full circles. With right sides together, layer the interfaced scoop fabric with a layer of non-interfaced fabric. The interfaced side will be the right side of the scoop. Cut out the circles.

Step 6: Using a smaller machine stitch and 1/4" seam, sew completely around the circle. Cut each circle in half. Clip seam allowances at small, regular intervals. Turn the scoops to the right side, striving for smooth curves, and press well. Top stitch each scoop with either straight or decorative stitching.

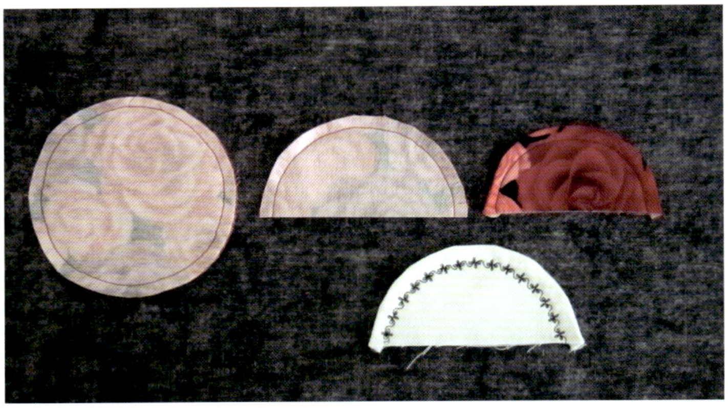

Sewing and finishing scoops.

Step 7: Make the tabs. Fuse light weight interfacing to half of the tab fabric. Layer, right sides together, the interfaced fabric with non-interfaced fabric. The interfaced side will be the right side of the tab. You will need one tab between each half-circle — for this project, 40. Cut the tabs and, using a smaller machine-stitch, stitch around the tab, leaving the bottom open. Clip curves, turn to the right side, and press well.

Sewing and finishing tabs.

Step 8: Create the binding assembly. Accurately measure the right side of the quilt top. To this measurement, add 2". Cut two attaching strips to exactly this measurement (in our example, 38"). Lay one of the strips on your work surface, right side up. Place a pin 1" in from either end and in the middle of the strip. Place a scoop, right side up, at either end with the edge aligned with the pin. Place a scoop at the middle, matching the middle of the scoop with that of the strip. Evenly place the rest of the scoops the length of the strip, pinning as you go. Insert a tab, right side up, behind and between each scoop. Match the tops of the tabs with the tops of the scoops, pinning as you go.

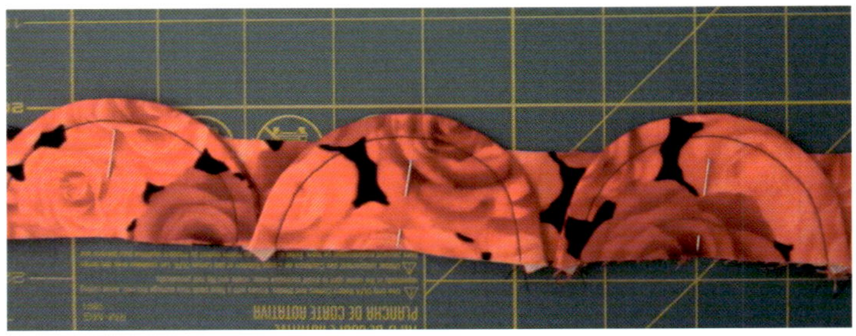

Place and pin scoops along attachment strip.

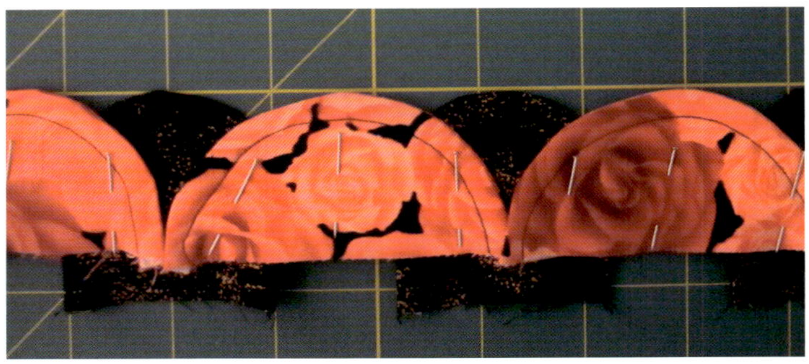

Insert and pin tabs.

Machine baste with a scant 1/4" seam.

Tip It's helpful to use a walking foot and position your needle three "ticks" to the right.

Machine baste the assembly.

Sew the second attachment strip to this assembly with right sides of the strip facing the right side of the scoops. Sew with a 1/4" seam allowance.

Tip Make sure your needle is in the center position.

Sew the second attachment strip to the assembly.

Trim excess tabs even with the seam allowance. Press both attachment strips away from the tabs.

The completed assembly.

Step 9: Pin right side of the border assembly attachment strip to the right side of the quilt top using a 1/2" seam allowance and making sure that your pins are right at the edge of the quilting line. Stitch in place. Trim the seam allowance to 1/4". Press away from the quilt top. On the back, turn under the edge of the attachment strip and stitch down by hand. The seam allowance from the quilt top and border assembly will completely fill the attachment strip. Repeat Steps 8 and 9 for the left side of the quilt.

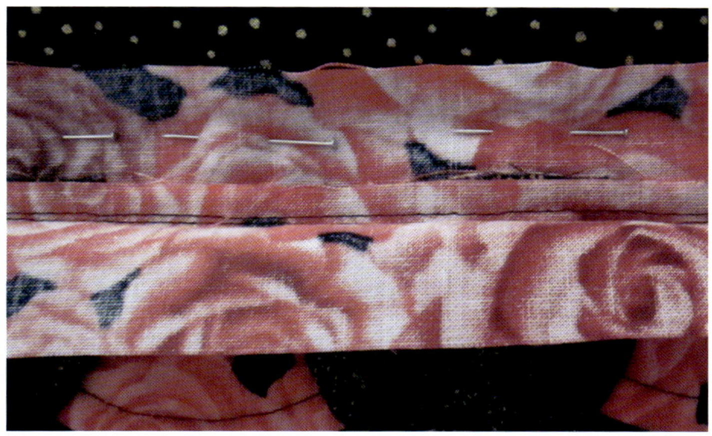

Pin the assembly to the quilt top and stitch as pinned.

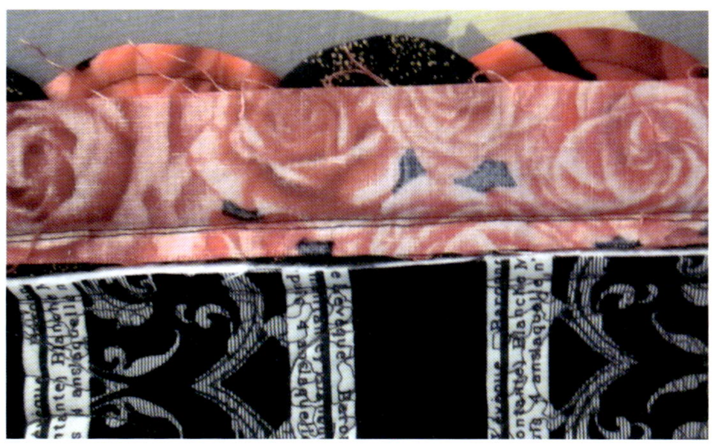

Trim the seam allowance to 1/4". The seam allowances nicely fill the attachment strips.

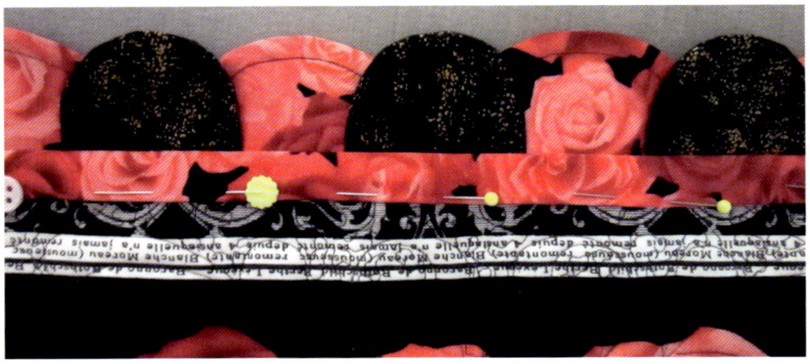

On the back, turn under the attachment strip and hand-stitch.

Step 10: Measure precisely the top of the quilt between the left and right side attachment strips. To this measurement, add 2". Cut two attachment strips this measurement. Prepare your binding assembly as in Step 8.

Step 11: Fold under 1/2" at both sides of the binding assembly. Pin the assembly, right sides together, to your quilt top, following the method described in Step 9. The folded edges of the binding assembly should encompass the edges of the side bindings. Stitch in place and trim the seam allowance. On the back, turn under the edge of the attachment strip and stitch down by hand. Stitch the ends of the binding assembly closed. Repeat Steps 10 and 11 for the bottom edge of the quilt.

The corner is encompassed by the attachment strip and hand-stitched closed.

Admire your accomplishment and be prepared to accept the accolades of your friends!

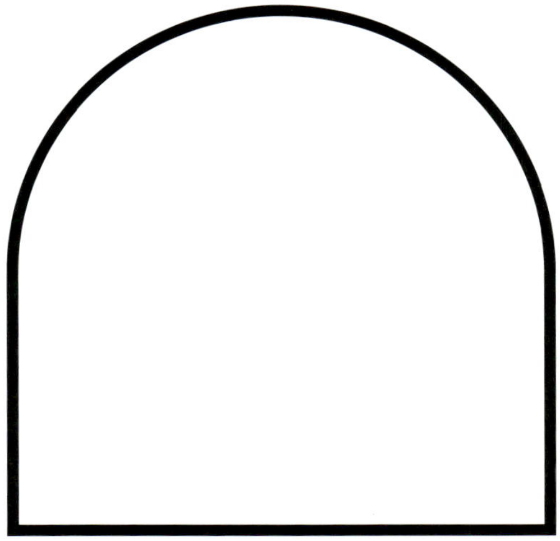

Pattern for edge finish tabs. Includes seam allowance.

Chapter Two:

Taupe Bouquet

When I received my first big quilt show award, I celebrated by buying a sizable collection of taupe fat quarters, the majority of them Daiwabo Fabrics from Japan. Over five ensuing years, I considered several different patterns to showcase the collection, but nothing seemed quite right. Finally, it all came together. A collection of silk dupioni, spotted in a quilt show vendor booth, was the perfect complement to my taupe collection. Two sets of vintage doilies were the perfect match. The smaller ones have a lovely tatted edge. In the larger, an embroidered linen ring is set off with crocheted centers and edging. Both of these doily sets whispered of their desire to be flowers set off by this collection of taupe cotton and silk.

Taupe Bouquet, 40" x 45". Quilted by Judy Taylor.

Working with Silk

Silk, when incorporated into quilts, adds a lovely sheen and texture. Viewers are impressed, especially when they know that silk, when it's worked, has a tendency to fray...badly. Here's the secret to working with silk for impressive and worry-free results.

Materials & Supplies

- Silk dupioni – fat quarters or cut yardage
- Shout® Color Catcher® sheets (recommended)
- Lightweight fusible interfacing

The Method

Step 1: Silk can successfully be combined with quilting cottons or used on their own for quilting with some preparation. Often, it is thought that silk must be dry-cleaned. Not so! The first cleaning treatment that is done with silk must then always be done with that fabric. Silk is washable!

Step 2: When your silk comes home, finish off the raw cut edges with a zigzag stitch. Warning: Skip this step and be prepared to have a lovely collection of silk thread after washing. Wash the silk with a small bit of mild detergent in cool to warm water. The use of a Shout Color Catcher sheet in the wash is highly recommended. Check the rinse water. If it is not running clear, repeat the washing until the silk has given up all of its excess dye. Do not skip this part of the process either! In my experience, silk gives up lots of dye. Managing this now will prevent dye running in your quilt.

Step 3: Once satisfied with the washing, tumble-dry on low heat until barely dry. The silk will come out quite wrinkled. Steam press the silk using the silk setting on your iron.

Step 4: When you are ready to cut your silk pieces, fuse lightweight interfacing to the wrong side of the silk, following the manufacturer's fusing instructions. It is not necessary to cover the entire fat quarter or yardage. Just prepare what you need.

Step 5: You can now treat the silk as you would quality quilting cottons. In *Taupe Bouquet*, each of the background blocks was created using four 1-1/2" strips of cotton and one 1-1/2" strip of silk. The placement of the silk in each block was varied to create interest. The blocks were (unfinished) 5-1/2" x 5-1/2". The blocks were set in an alternating orientation for added visual interest, finishing at 5" x 5".

The Pattern – Favorite Leaf

This is my favorite leaf shape and I use it in many quilts. Some of the leaves in *Taupe Bouquet* are accented by a silk inset. Here's how!

Materials & Supplies

- Green silk, washed and pressed with lightweight interfacing fused on wrong side
- Green cotton fabric
- Card stock or template plastic
- Fine line Sharpie® marking pen
- Fabric glue
- Toothpick or bamboo skewer

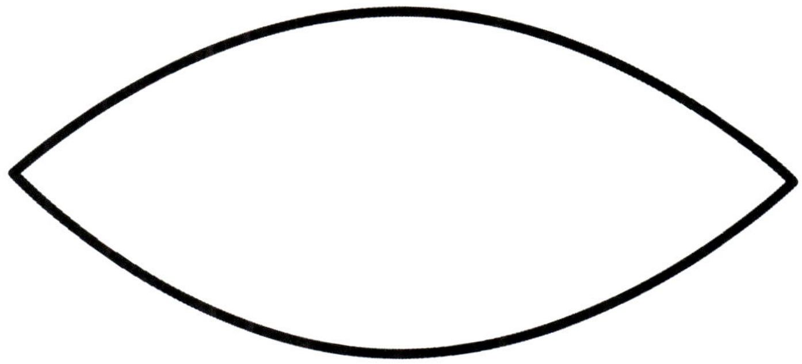

Favorite leaf pattern. Pattern is actual size and does not include any turn under allowance.

The Method

Piece prepared silk and quilting cotton.

Step 1: Cut strips of prepared silk 3/4" wide and strips of green cotton at 2-1/2" wide. Using an accurate 1/4" seam, piece the silk between the cotton strips. Press well, with seams allowances pressed toward the cotton.

Step 2: Create pattern templates. Trace leaf patterns on card stock or template plastic. Carefully cut out the templates. Templates are actual size and do not include seam allowances.

Step 3: Trace patterns on the wrong side of lightweight fusible interfacing using the Sharpie marking pen. Carefully cut on the marked lines.

Fuse interfacing leaves to wrong side of silk/cotton strip set.

Step 4: Lay the fusible leaves on the wrong side of the green fabric. Make sure that leaves are on the bias (to help with the turn under) and that there's sufficient space between leaves. Following the manufacturer's instructions, fuse the leaves in place.

Clip edges, turn under, and glue seam allowances in place.

Finished leaf is ready to be appliquéd to your quilt top.

Step 5: Adding a generous 1/4" turn under allowance, cut out each leaf. Clip curved edges at 1/4" intervals. Using fabric glue and a toothpick or bamboo skewer, glue the turn under allowance to the back of the leaf.

Machine appliqué using open toe foot, blind hem stitch, clear thread on top, and matching thread in the bobbin.

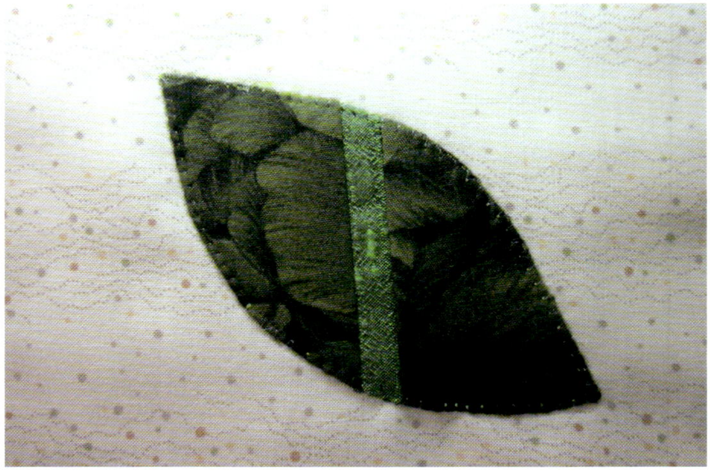

Finished machine appliqué.

Step 6: Attach your machine's open toe foot and thread clear poly thread in the top and thread to match the appliqué in the bobbin. Set your machine for a blind hem stitch, reducing the width and length of the stitch. Position the appliqué piece on the quilt top, pinning to hold in place if necessary. Stitch so that the presser foot rides just along the appliqué piece. The straight stitches will lie just along the appliqué piece in the background and the left-right stitches will catch the edge of the appliqué, securely attaching it.

You've added a bit of sheen and lots of interest to your appliqué leaves. Impressive!

Chapter 3:

Camille's Butterfly

Camille has been my friend for over twenty-five years. She's loyal, supportive, understanding, fun, and everything a good friend should be. Camille loves purple, good wine, and anything with butterflies — that makes shopping for birthday and holiday gifts extremely easy!

This yellow vintage linen was a two-parter: the larger piece was accompanied by one small matching coaster. The larger piece whispered of spring, flowers, and butterflies. The design elements of the linen are accented with the addition of fabric paints. The modern fabrics in the piece blend well with the vintage charm of the doily. Hating to be separated from its larger friend, the small coaster lives on the back of the quilt as the label.

Camille's Butterfly, 27-3/4" x 24-3/4"

Machine Embroidered "Ribbon" Border Trim

Want to break up a border and add a bit of pizzaz? Create your own "ribbon" trim with this fun and easy technique.

Materials & Supplies

- Fabric for "ribbon"
- Spray starch or Mary Ellen's Best Press™
- Rayon machine embroidery thread to match "ribbon" fabric
- Tear-away stabilizer

The Method

Step 1: Determine the width of ribbon you want to create. In the example project, the fabric strip is 1" wide. Cut strips of fabric double the desired finished width, in this case 2"-wide strips. If you need strips that are longer than the width of the fabric, piece strips using 45 degree angles to reduce bulk.

Step 2: Lightly press the fabric strip in half with wrong sides together. Bring both raw edges in to the center pressed mark. Press well, using a light misting of spray starch or Mary Ellen's Best Press.

Step 3: Pin the prepared fabric strip in place on the right side of the border fabric. Cut strips of tear-away stabilizer wide enough to extend beyond the width of the fabric ribbon. Pin the stabilizer behind the assembled border and ribbon fabric.

Fabric ribbon with straight stitching on the left and decorative stitching on the right.

Step 4: Using matching rayon machine embroidery thread in the top and matching cotton thread in the bobbin, stitch close to the folded edges on both sides of the ribbon using a straight stitch.

Step 5: Select a decorative stitch on your machine. Stitches that have areas of solid fill work best. In the sample, the stitch is a series of triangle points. When adding the decorative stitch, the goal is to cover the running stitch and edge of the fabric. Stitching up a few quick samples will allow you to select the one that you like the best; adjust the width and length of the stitches (if necessary) and check for balanced tension. Once you've made your choice and tested a sample, use the running stitch as a guide and stitch along both edges with the decorative stitch.

Step 6: Carefully remove the tear-away stabilizer. Attach your border strips to the body of the quilt.

The color and design possibilities here are endless. For the decorative machine embroidery, consider thread colors that complement or contrast with your selected ribbon fabric. When you quilt your piece, quilting a straight stitch close to the edge of the machine embroidery will add a bit of dimension to the ribbon. You might also consider a small quilting pattern over the "ribbon" to change its look. Or, how about adding other embellishments, such as beading or couched threads, to further enhance the "ribbon" look and feel. The sky is the limit!

Doily as Quilt Label

What were those small doilies used for? Imagine beautiful water or wine goblets resting upon them, complementing place settings of china and silver. Today, these small treasures can be used for quilt labels to complement the doily appearing on the front!

Materials & Supplies

- Small "coaster-size" doily
- Light box or bright window
- Painter's tape
- Label text, sized and printed out on paper
- Fine line permanent marker, such as Micron® or Sharpie® brand

The Method

Step 1: Measure the area on the doily where you will write your label information. Using your computer's word processing program, set your margins to this usable space.

Step 2: Using a plain font in as large a size as possible, type out the information you would like on the label. Include the name of the quilt, its maker, the year it was made, and where it was made. If you have information about the doily (i.e., doily ca. 1941 made by Bernice Abbott nee Prusa), include that if you have the space. Print out the information.

Tape the printed pattern guide and doily to the surface of a light table or sunny window.

Step 3: Using painter's tape, tape the label information to the light box or to a bright, sunny window. Center the doily over this and tape that down as well.

Step 4: With the printed information as a guide, use the fine-line permanent marker to write the text on the doily.

Tip Use a light touch. Doilies are often made of looser weave fabric and the ink may run a bit. A lighter touch will help control ink bleed.

Step 5: Pin your label to the lower left-hand corner of your finished quilt back and hand-stitch in place.

Doily label stitched in place.

The doilies we find are often anonymous, made by women whose names and stories are lost to time. Don't let that happen with your quilts! Always include a label so future admirers will at least know your name and where you lived. Labeling your quilts buys you a small measure of immortality!

Chapter 4:

Lynn's Broderie Perse

My friend Lynn has been involved in the quilt industry for over thirty years. She is an author, teacher, guild founder, designer, quilt show director, and the list goes on and on. Several years ago, she gifted me with a vintage fabric panel with two printed squares. Knowing of my interest in vintage linens, she hoped that I would find it inspiring. How to honor this vintage fabric was a puzzle, until a cream colored doily with a beautiful crochet edge whispered, "Use me with the vintage panel." A perfect result!

Lynn's Broderie Perse, 21" x 21"

Color Copies and Digital Images as Design Aids

Afraid to cut into precious, one-of-a-kind or vintage fabric? These design tips will help you plan and decide before taking a snip. While my goal was appliqué with elements from my vintage panel, this technique can be used for multiple purposes.

Materials & Supplies

- Color copier – either a home version or a quick visit to your local copy shop
- Digital camera – Your smart phone camera will work as well

The Method

Step 1: Make color copies of the elements or bits of your precious fabric that you would like to use. Making several copies increases your options.

Try various combinations ...

... of your elements ...

... until you find ...

... the one you ...

... like the best!

Step 2: From the copies, cut out the design elements. Using the paper versions, audition a combination. If you have made more than one copy of an element, make sure that you are not trying more of those elements in paper than you have in fabric. Take a digital photo of the combination.

Step 3: Rearrange the paper elements into a new configuration. Take a digital photo of the new combination. Repeat this process until you feel you have exhausted your design possibilities and you have several different photos.

Step 4: Review the photos and select the layout that is most pleasing to you. You can do this by flipping through the photos on your camera or smart phone. You can also download them into your computer for a side by side comparison. Another option is to print them out. Use the method that works best for you.

Step 5: Cut your precious fabric with confidence! You are assured that there will be no mistakes and no regrets.

Easy Fusible Broderie Perse

"Broderie perse" is a style of appliqué using printed elements to create a design on background fabric. Here's an easy, fusible technique that finishes by machine.

Materials & Supplies

- Fabric with printed elements that will create your design
- Lightweight fusible web, such as Steam A Seam®, Steam a Seam 2®, or Mistyfuse™
- Small, sharp detail scissors
- Background fabric
- Ironing surface and iron
- Thread to stitch appliqué

The Method

Step 1: Following the manufacturer's instructions for your fusible product of choice, apply fusible webbing to the wrong side of the fabric elements you will cut out.

Press fusible web to the wrong side of selected motifs and carefully cut them out.

Step 2: Carefully cut the design elements from the fabric. Arrange them on your background base.

Step 3: Following the manufacturer's instructions on your fusible product of choice, fuse the elements in place.

Step 4: Stitch around the raw edges to secure the appliqué. There are several ways of doing this. Two are explained here:

A. Thread your sewing machine with poly monofilament on top and thread to match the color of the appliqué piece in the bobbin. Using either a small blind hem stitch or zigzag stitch, sew around all the raw edges. The advantage of this method is that the stitching is not noticeable, other than a bit of sheen from the monofilament. This was the method used in the sample project, *Lynn's Broderie Perse.*

B. Stitch around each of the appliqué elements using your machine's blanket stitch. Select thread to match the appliqué or use a contrasting thread, depending upon the look you prefer. For photography, contrasting thread was used for greater visibility. Follow these instructions to achieve a Better Blanket Stitch:

- Set your machine for "needle down" and use an open toe foot.
- Begin by bringing your bobbin thread up to the surface.

Beginning machine blanket stitch.

- Make sure that your needle falls just to the right of the motif.
- The "left-right" stitches should be perpendicular to the edge of the fabric. When going around curves, adjust the fabric position when the needle is on the right.

Blanket stitch from the right side with contrasting thread for visibility.

- To give a nice finish to interior corners, follow these steps:

1. Make sure your last left-right stitch ends with the needle down right at the corner, which becomes your "pivot point."
2. Raise the presser foot and turn your work so that the foot is at a 90 degree angle to the corner.
3. Lower the presser foot and take one-half stitch (the needle comes up). Raise the presser foot and reposition the work so the needle will re-enter the fabric at the pivot point. Lower the presser foot and complete the stitch. The needle will be down and at the pivot point.
4. Complete the left-right stitch, which will end with the needle down at the pivot point.
5. Raise the presser foot and turn the work so that the foot is at a 90 degree angle to the next segment you're going to stitch.

6. Lower the presser foot and take one-half stitch (the needle comes up). Raise the presser foot and reposition the work so that the needle will re-enter the fabric at the pivot point. Lower the presser foot and complete the stitch; your needle will be down and at the pivot point.
7. Complete the left-right stitch and keep sewing.
8. This method gives corners a three-stitch finish, just as if the stitching were done by hand.

- When you have stitched around the motif, finish with 2-3 very small stitches in place.

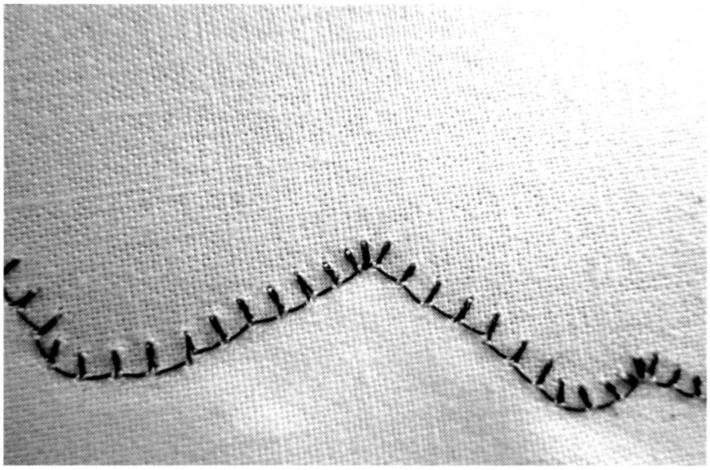

Blanket stitch on the wrong side with contrasting thread for visibility.

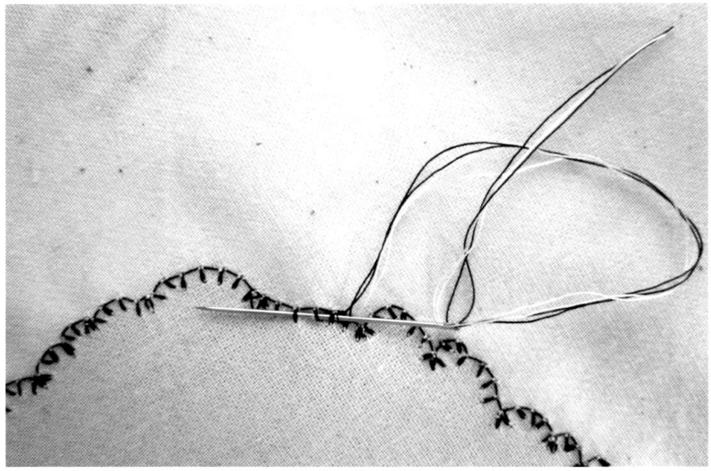

Pull in threads for a neat finish.

- Pull the three thread tails from the top of the work to the back.
- Thread all four thread tails onto your needle, take a small tack stitch, and run the threads through a few stitches on the back for a neat and secure finish. Clip the threads close to your work.

You can now manage broderie perse using these easy methods. Your design possibilities have increased tremendously!

Chapter 5:

Janet's Dream

I had the great pleasure of interviewing Janet, a top quilt show prize winner. In addition to being an award-winning quilter of extraordinary talent, Janet is a professional picture framer, a job she has held since high school. When this small chemical-lace edged doily whispered that there was no need to quilt everything, Janet guided my conversations with my local framer and graciously gave permission to share her knowledge here.

Janet's Dream, 27" x 21"

Adding Words to Doilies

Sometimes the large open areas of doilies just beg for the inclusion of a word or name. Here's how "Dream" was added to this doily, along with other ideas for the addition of text to your doilies.

Materials & Supplies

- Doily with tightly-woven fabric center
- Appropriately-size printout of a word to add to the doily
- Light box or sunny window
- Sharp #2 pencil
- Painter's tape
- Jacquard® Textile Color paint
- Fine-line paint brush

The Method

Step 1: Determine the word you would like to add to your doily. The word used in the sample project is "Dream"; other possibilities might be Peace, Believe, Love, Family, etc.

Step 2: Measure the area of your doily that will accommodate the word. In the word processing program on your computer, set your margins to these measurements. Type your selected word in the center of the box. Adjust for font selection and size to fill the space. Once you settle on a selection, print it out on paper.

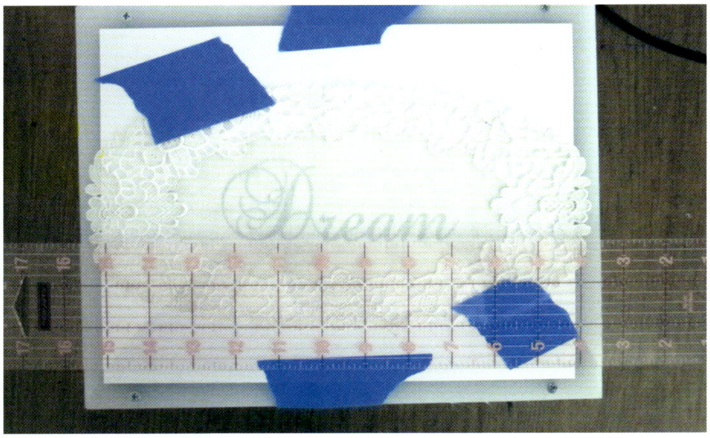

Tape the printed word and doily to a light box or sunny window, making sure it is straight.

Step 3: With the painter's tape, tape the paper image to your light box or on a sunny window. Center the doily over the image, making sure that the space is pleasingly filled and that the word will be straight on the doily. Tape the doily in place with painter's tape.

TIP Don't care for any of the fonts available on your computer? Search the internet for "font image generator." You will find several sites that allow you to enter words, try different fonts and sizes, and download the image you select to your computer. Most of the sites offer quick start tutorials on how to use the services; many are free of charge. The sample project was created using a free internet font image generator.

Lightly trace the word with a hard lead pencil.

Dream painted on vintage chemical lace doily.

TIP If you do not care for the idea of painting, there are lots of other ways to add text to your vintage doilies. Here are a few other ideas:

- If you have an embroidery machine and/or design software, use your machine's capabilities or digitize your work and stitch it out, following the manufacturer's instructions for stabilizing the work.
- Hand-embroider the word with a combination of satin and back stitches — or any stitches that will achieve the look you want.
- Use permanent markers, such as Micron® pens. Be aware that ink may bleed out into the fabric fibers. If choosing this method, look for a doily with a tightly woven fabric base, use a light touch, and work carefully.
- Turn your word into a fusible appliqué element and fuse to the doily. If you are framing your piece, there should be no need to stitch around the appliqué.
- Use Lesley Riley's Transfer Artist Paper (TAP®) to transfer words to your doily. Write your desired word(s) in the font of your choice in your word processing program on your computer. Reverse the image of that text and print onto the TAP with an inkjet printer. By simply using a hot iron, you can transfer those words to the doily. Complete instructions for the use of TAP are included with the product (see Resources List).

Step 4: Using a hard lead pencil, lightly trace the outline of the word on to the doily. Remove the doily.

Step 5: Using Jacquard Textile Colors and a fine line paintbrush, paint the word on the doily. Once the paint is dry, heat set.

Framing Textiles

Who says all fiber art needs to be quilted and bound? While a project like *Janet's Dream* might look lovely quilted and turned into a pillow or wall hanging, this delicate doily just begged to be framed. The background fabric — a swirling, celestial print — complements the theme and helps set a mood when hung in the bedroom. Following most of Janet's advice about framing, here is how I prepared the piece.

Materials & Supplies

- Acid free foam core board, cut to desired size
- Background fabric, cut to desired size (to cover surface of foam core board)
- SpraynBond™ Fusible Adhesive spray
- Prepared doily
- Needle and thread (Select a needle that can pierce the foam core. I used cotton thread.)
- Iron and ironing surface.

The Method

Step 1: Find the center of the background fabric and the center of the doily. Following the manufacturer's instructions, spray the back of the doily with SpraynBond Fusible Adhesive. When the adhesive is dry, place in the center of the background fabric and fuse.

Step 2: Test the bond around the edges. If there are areas that are not well-fused, stitch those in place by hand using thread that matches the doily and small stitches.

Step 3: Center the background fabric on the acid free foam core board. Using a needle and thread, and with a running stitch, sew the background fabric to the foam core. Strive to keep the background fabric smooth and taut. Keep the stitches about 1/4" from the edge of the foam core board. They will later be covered by the frame.

Hand-stitching on reverse of foam core board.

Step 4: Take your piece to your professional framer. Discuss the framing with him/her, covering these points:

- Matting for your piece...or not. What color do you want the matting to be? In what shape should the mat opening be cut? How much of the background fabric do you want to show? In *Janet's Dream*, the visible background fabric creates a two inch border around the doily. Do you want a single or a double mat? A double mat would create another area of color. In the sample project, there is a single mat. Because mat board is cut with a bevel, it appears that there is an ivory oval. This effect could be created with a second mat board. Just to add one more option, your frame shop should also be able to cover mat board with the fabric of your choice. If that is your preference, bring your fabric with you and explore this option with your framer. If you prefer not to have your piece matted, that is perfectly all right. If you opt for no mat, Janet recommends asking the framer to put a glass spacer in the frame to hold the glass off the surface of the doily. If you have decided to use a mat, these are not necessary because the mat holds the glass off the doily's surface.

- Mat spacers...or not. Do you want the mat to rest directly on top of the background? If you'd like to add a feeling of depth, ask the framer to raise the mat up with 1/8" foam core board.

- The frame itself. The sample project's frame is painted wood. There are many options available, from sleek metals to ornately carved wood. Sometimes, framing elements can be layered to create even more options. The framer will have lots of samples and suggestions and help you choose.

- The glass for the frame. Janet recommended conservation glass, which comes in either a regular or non-glare variety. It blocks about 97 percent of ultra violet light, which will keep your piece from fading. Janet also suggested that I avoid the non-glare option, feeling that its matte finish reduces the clarity of what is seen through it. Your frame shop should have samples of both to help you envision the end result. The sample project uses regular conservation glass.

Ready for a visit to the professional framer.

Professional framing can be expensive, but the results are worth the cost. After all, it is art that will be displayed in your home for years to come. Many framers offer sales and discount coupons, so take advantage of those. I cut the cost of framing *Janet's Dream* by using a 60 percent off coupon and achieved considerable savings. Have fun exploring framing as an option for displaying your fiber art creations.

Chapter 6:

Janice's Cardinal

My mother's neighbor, Janice, had planned to make a quilt from denim squares cut from old, used jeans and overalls. When she realized she would never complete the project, she offered the squares to me, hoping that I would "do something" with them. When I found this lovely vintage doily with embroidered floral motif, it whispered to me that it was a perfect match for the denim and suggested that red accents would set it off beautifully.

Janice's Cardinal, 22-3/4" x 22-3/4"

Working with Denim or Upholstery Fabrics

Using denim or upholstery fabrics in quilt projects adds texture and interest. These heavier fabrics also create some challenges. If one uses the quilter's 1/4" seam to sew heavier fabrics together, the bulk of that seam creates visible ridges in the top. Here is a method that reduces that bulk and results in a nice, flat quilt top.

Materials & Supplies

- Denim or upholstery fabric squares. (The sample project used nine squares cut at 6" x 6".)
- Lightweight muslin for base fabric. (For the sample project, a 20" x 20" piece was used)
- 3/8" wide ribbon to cover joins. (Project sample required 2-1/4 yards.)

The Method

Step 1: Make sure that the fabric squares are cut accurately with straight edges and corners at 90 degree angles. This is important so the edges and corners butt together snuggly.

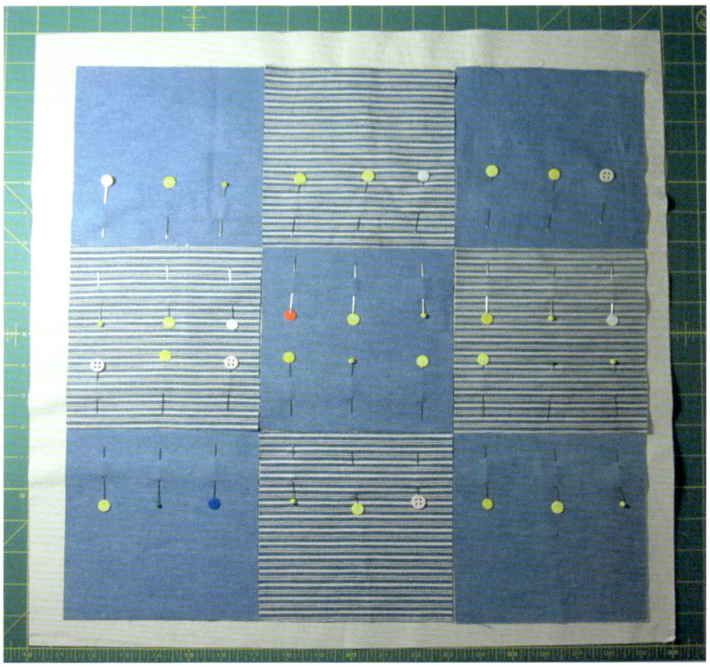

Lay denim squares on the muslin base, making sure corners and edges match snuggly, and pin in place.

Step 2: Lay out the background squares on top of the muslin base. Ensure that the edges and corners match with no gaps and no overlap. Pin heavily along all joins.

Step 3: Set your sewing machine for the zigzag stitch. Increase the width of the stitch to the largest size and decrease the stitch length. You need wide, tight stitches, but a satin stitch effect is not required. Stitch along all fabric joins, making sure to catch all raw edges with the stitching.

Zigzag stitch over abutted edges in both directions.

TIP If your project calls for appliquéing a doily on top of the created base and the background shadows through, consider trimming the background from behind the doily if there is no cutwork in the doily.

Step 4: Cover the joins with ribbon. On the sewing machine, ribbon was stitched at both sides over the joins. Change the look by using grosgrain rather than satin ribbon or use ribbon with pattern. You now have a nice, flat top with no thick bumps to quilt over.

Alternate Option – Don't care for the look of the ribbon covering the joins? When stitching your joins together, set your machine to satin stitch length and zigzag the joins together. This creates a different look, which you can make subtle by using matching thread or an additional design feature by using contrasting or variegated thread.

Rick-rack Border Insert

A rick-rack insert between the center of the quilt and its border adds a pop of color and textural interest. The goal is to have the bumps of one side of the rick-rack be visible and fall right at the seam line. Here is how it's done.

Materials & Supplies

- Rick-rack — 5/8" wide (0.625"/15.875mm)

NOTE If you are buying in 3-yard packages, calculate how many pieces you can cut from one package. You can also find this in 9-yard rolls or by the yard. Just remember that you will need to have a continuous piece of rick-rack for each side.

The Method

Step 1: Square up your quilt top; in the project sample, it was squared to 18" x 18". Cut four lengths of rick-rack — one for each side — 2" longer than the side measurement. In the project, four 20" lengths were cut.

Machine baste rick-rack trim to the quilt edge.

Step 2: Align the top of the rick-rack bumps with the raw edge of the fabric. Machine baste first to the top and bottom and then to the right and left sides.

TIP Use your machine's walking foot and use the 1/4" seam guide. Set the needle position 2-3 positions to the right of center.

Step 3: Trim the ends of the rick-rack even with the corners of the quilt top.

Perfectly placed rick-rack insert.

Step 4: Attach the border fabric strips. Matching the raw edge of the border strip with the raw edge of the quilt top, stitch the top and bottom borders. Use your machine's walking foot and the 1/4" seam guide. Stitch with the needle one position to the right of center. Press the seam toward the border.

Step 5: Repeat Step 4 for the right and left hand side borders. Again, use your machine's walking foot and the 1/4" seam guide with the needle positioned one position to the right of center. Press the seam toward the border.

When quilting your project, take care not to catch the rick-rack in with the quilting stitches. You want those bumps to remain loose and free. I have used this technique on several quilts. It is easy and impressive when done, adding interest and an unexpected pop of color. Try it!

Chapter 7:

Leah's Sunny Sunflowers

Patti is not only my grant writing business partner, she is also my friend. Her daughter, Leah, used to house-sit for us when we traveled. Leah is grown now and a Master's level, bilingual speech therapist. She recently married and carried sunflowers in her bouquet. She and her new husband, Nick, received a quilt with sunflowers to mark their wedding. The vintage linen in this piece came to me all white. The flowers around the outer edge whispered that they longed to look like Leah's sunflowers. A few touches of paint, sunflower print fabric, and Dresden Plate appliqué makes this project sunny sunflowers indeed!

Leah's Sunny Sunflowers, 29" x 33-1/2". Quilted by Judy Taylor.

Dresden Plate Appliqué

Dresden Plate blocks make wonderful flowers! Dresden Plate blocks are made by sewing twenty wedge segments into a circle. No matter how large or small the wedge segments are, the center circle remains the same size. For an even more interesting look, you can layer plates of different sizes. It is a versatile block you will want in your quilter's toolkit.

Materials & Supplies

- Scraps of yellow for the petals of the sunflowers
- Scrap of brown for sunflower center
- Heat-resistant template plastic
- Spray starch or Mary Ellen's Best Press™

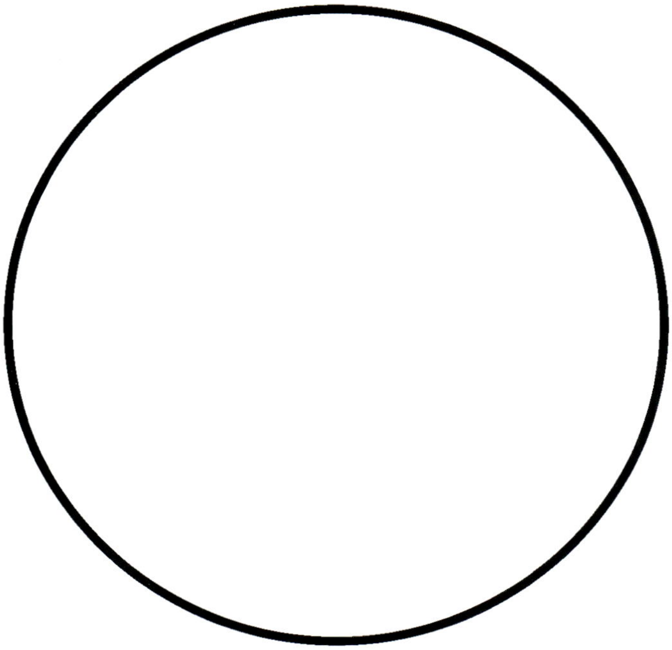

Pattern for Dresden Plate Center. Pattern is actual size and does not include any turn under allowance.

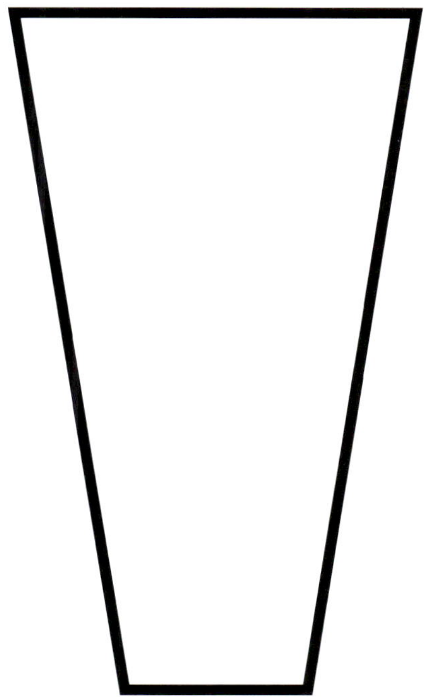

Wedge pattern for 9" Dresden Plates.

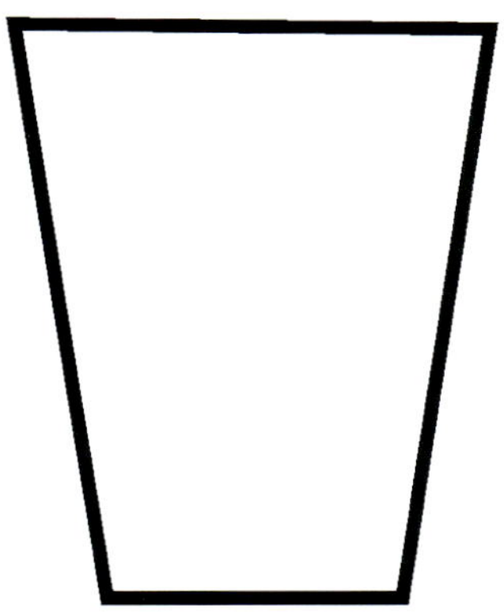

Wedge pattern for 6-1/2" Dresden Plates.

NOTE A variety of values and careful value placement will provide a look of light falling on the flower.

The Method

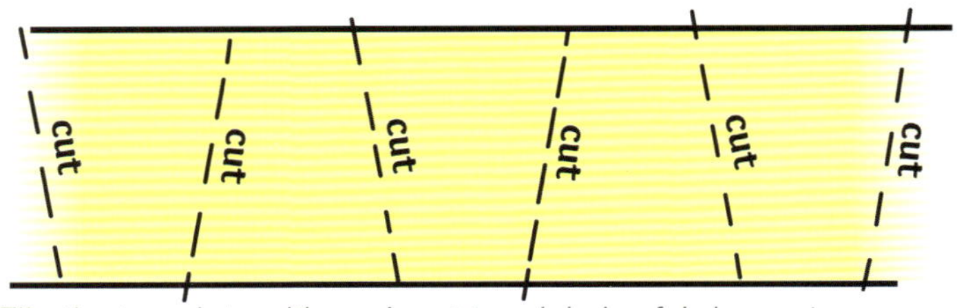

Flip the template with each cut to minimize fabric waste.

TIP The sides of your wedges will be on the bias. Minimize handling and stretching of these edges!

Sew wider ends of wedges and clip seam allowances.

Pressed wedges ready to be joined.

Step 1: Cut 20 wedges for sunflower petals using one of the templates provided. The smaller template will make a sunflower about 6-1/2" in diameter and the larger a flower about 9". To get the most out of your fabric, cut scraps into 2" wide strips for the smaller and 3-1/2" wide strips for the larger flower. Nestle the template first one way and then the other, cutting wedges.

Step 2: Fold wedges in half lengthwise with right sides facing. Reduce the length of your sewing machine stitch. Sew across the widest edge with a 1/4" seam. Save time by chain piecing the wedges.

Step 3: Being careful not to clip into the stitching, trim a wedge out of each seam allowance at the fold. Finger press the seam open and turn the fabric to the wrong side. Press well, taking care not to stretch the edges of the wedge.

Seam wedges by stitching in reverse to the edge and then forward to complete the seam.

Step 4: Lay out the 20 wedges in a circle. Select two wedges and place them right sides together. Begin stitching by starting 1/4" down from the top of the wedge and stitching in reverse to the edge. Now, stitch in the normal direction to the end of the wedge. This prevents having little thread ends at the edge of your plate. Continue joining wedges until all 20 have been joined.

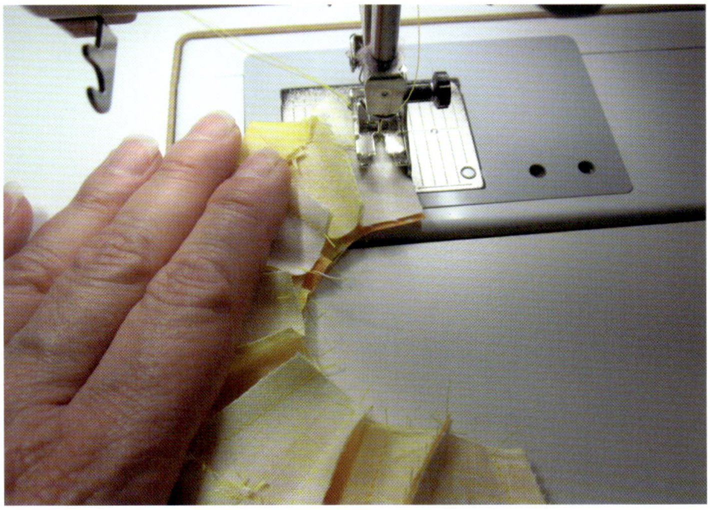

The final seam completes the circle.

Step 5: Fold the plate in half with the two remaining right-side edges facing. Complete the last seam to join all into a circle. Finger-press the seam open. Press well, using steam if needed, so that the circle lies flat and keeps its circular shape.

Completed plate.

TIP Make sure you are using heat-resistant plastic! You will be pressing over the template and do not want a melty mess!

Step 6: Make the sunflower center. Using the template provided, trace this shape onto heat-resistant template plastic.

Running stitch around the outside of the flower center.

Gather around the center template and tie off the ends.

Step 7: Cut a circle of brown fabric a generous 1/4" larger than the template. Using a needle and thread, take small running stitches all around the outer edge of the fabric circle. Holding the plastic template in the center, pull up the threads to turn the seam allowance over the edge of the plastic. Tie off the thread ends.

Step 8: Using spray starch, spritz the fabric and press well with the plastic template inside. Allow to cool and set. Pop the template out of the fabric and dry press again. Leave the gathering threads in place.

Pin the sunflower plate and center into position.

Machine appliqué the center.

Stitch around the edges of the plate with a straight stitch.

Step 9: Position your yellow sunflower plate on the background fabric and pin each wedge. Position the center brown circle over the opening in the plates. Check that the piece is centered and pin. Using polyester monofilament thread (either clear or smoke) in the top and brown thread in the bobbin, machine appliqué the center down. The traditional method of sewing plates down is with a straight stitch 1/4" from the edge of the outer tips. This method was used in the sample project. If you prefer, you may hand or machine appliqué the outer edges down and add the look of traditional application with quilting.

You now have a method to make charming Dresden Plate flowers. They need not always be sunflowers; petals of other colors with yellow centers work well too. If you would like to make other size plates, increasing your design possibilities, consider buying EZ Quilting® Easy Dresden ruler by Darlene Zimmerman. For use with your rotary cutter, it is a ruler that really works!

Sunflower Leaf Appliqué

Sunflower leaves are somewhat heart-shaped. Use this template to finish off your sunny sunflowers nicely.

TIP These directions are for my preferred method of preparing and handling appliqué. Step-by-step photos appear in Chapter 2. Use the method you prefer, remembering that the sunflower leaf template is provided at actual size.

Materials & Supplies

- Template plastic or card stock
- Scraps of green fabric
- Lightweight fusible interfacing
- Ultra fine line Sharpie® marker
- Fabric glue stick
- Toothpicks or bamboo skewers

The Method

Step 1: Create template. Trace the leaf template onto card stock or template plastic. Carefully cut along traced lines. The template does not include a seam allowance.

Step 2: Trace leaf shapes onto the wrong side of lightweight fusible interfacing using the Sharpie marker. Carefully cut along traced lines.

Step 3: Fuse leaf-shaped interfacing to the wrong side of the green leaf fabric. Make sure to place the interfacing leaves on the bias and allow sufficient space around shapes for the addition of seam allowances. Following manufacturer's instructions, fuse in place. Cut each leaf out, adding a 1/4" seam allowance. Clip around the entire seam allowance at scant 1/4" intervals. Be sure to cut down into the valley between the halves.

Step 4: Using the glue stick and toothpicks or skewers, glue the seam allowance under all around the leaf. Allow to dry. Place on background fabric and machine appliqué in place.

Pattern for sunflower leaf. Pattern is actual size and does not include any turn under allowance.

No Math Fabric-Changing Binding

Wonder where the binding is on *Leah's Sunny Sunflowers*? It's there — it's just not quite so noticeable because the binding fabric matches the background fabric all the way around the quilt. The binding is one continuous fabric strip. Here is how it's done...without any complex math!

Materials & Supplies

- Binding strips: Cut 2-1/2" wide and with the grain of sufficient length to cover matching areas on the quilt top

The Method

Step 1: Do not join fabric bits together. However, prepare them by folding in half, length-wise, with wrong sides together and press. Make sure all ends are cut at 90 degree angles.

Measure 1/4" beyond the quilt background seam and trim.

Step 2: Begin in a large area with room to accommodate your finishing binding join. Make sure that when you start sewing the binding on, you leave at least an 8" tail free for this join. On the sample project, I began the binding on the bottom in the brown area. Sew the binding in place, mitering any corners as you come to them. Stop several inches before a fabric change. Accurately measure the distance from where you stopped sewing to the seam where the background fabric changes. To that measurement, add 1/4". Cut the binding at that point straight across.

Join binding with 1/4" seam allowance.

Step 3: Using a 1/4" seam allowance, join the next fabric. To reduce bulk, press the seam open. Continue sewing, mitering corners as you come to them. Repeat this process as fabric changes occur.

Press binding seams open to reduce bulk.

Continue sewing the binding.

Step 4: When arriving back at the beginning, join the binding strips using your usual technique and complete the binding attachment. Turn the binding to the back of the quilt and finish by hand or machine.

Binding ready to be turned to the back of the quilt. The fabric change binding extends the visual field of the top.

This binding method takes a bit of extra time and planning, but extends the visual field of the quilt, eliminating the stopping point that a traditional, one-fabric binding often creates. If you have a variety of fabric changes around your quilt top and puzzle over what fabric to use for binding, consider this fabric changing binding technique as the solution to that challenge!

Chapter 8:

Aunt Lydia's Autumn

Aunt Lydia, one of my mother's older sisters, always treated me as her favorite niece. She was an extraordinary knitter and celebrated a November birthday. My birthday, as well as my mother's, is in October, which made our Midwestern autumn season all the more special. The changing colors of the leaves, pumpkins on front porches, and a crispness in the air are things I miss now that I live in the Arizona desert. The doily here was crocheted by Aunt Lydia probably in the 1940s. This doily, with its ivory and orange thread, whispered to me that it would happily be joined with a lovely pumpkin to celebrate my favorite time of year.

Aunt Lydia's Autumn, 29" x 25". Quilted by Terri Doyle.

Changing Fabric Value with Sheer Overlay

Having trouble finding the perfect fabric? For *Aunt Lydia's Autumn*, I found a lovely autumn print that I thought might look like vintage wallpaper. It would have been perfect if the colors had been just a bit more muted. Here is how to change the value of a fabric with the use of sheer overlay.

Materials & Supplies

- Background fabric
- Sheer fabrics in a variety of colors. (For the sample project, I auditioned three different colors of silk organza.)

The Method

TIP While the sample project features silk organza, you can also use polyester organza, bridal illusion, netting, or tulle. Care needs to be taken in pressing some of these selections. Test a scrap to find the right iron temperature, and make sure to protect your overlay with a pressing cloth. You may have to protect the overlay with a pressing cloth throughout your project's construction and finishing. Also, if your project will be washed, I recommend stitching a sample and then washing and drying, as you would like to be able to. This test may lead you to make another selection.

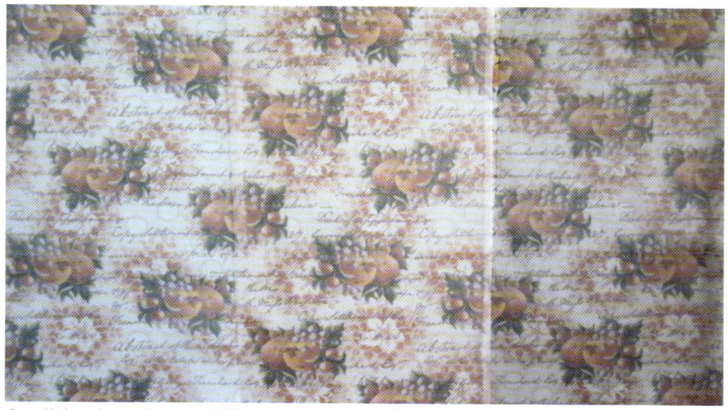

Auditioning three different colors of silk organza — ivory, apricot, and cocoa.

Original fabric.

Step 1: Pin your pre-washed and pressed background fabric to a design wall or tape it up on a solid surface.

Step 2: Pin a selection of sheer fabric over the background. Try single and double layers.

TIP Using an overlay further increases design possibilities when you entrap items between the background layer and the overlay. The possibilities are endless, from bits of shiny threads to snippets of fabric, to beads and sequins. To keep entrapped items where you'd like them (in other words, so they don't all just fall to the bottom of the sandwich), sew a grid — either geometric or free form — to help hold entrapped bits.

Two layers of the ivory silk organza provided the softness wanted for the project.

Step 3: Evaluate and choose which you will use. This is where a digital camera or smart phone can come in handy. Things often look different through the camera lens and it offers a different perspective. When I auditioned my three fabric selections, this helped me determine that the apricot was too orange, the cocoa was too dark, but the ivory was just right.

Step 4: Cut background fabric and sheer overlay to the desired size. Heavily pin through the entire piece to keep the overlay from shifting. Machine baste around all sides close to the raw edge. Remove pins. You can now treat this as one fabric. In the sample project, the entire background behind the feature design was overlaid with two layers of ivory silk organza.

Step 5: Complete the quilt top, taking care when pressing over the overlay. Layer and quilt as you usually would.

If you have or find a fabric that would be perfect "if only," consider using an overlay to change its value. Lighter overlays make for a lighter value, while darker overlays do the opposite. Experiment and make your fabrics be exactly what you want them to be!

Coffee-dyeing Cotton Trim

Aunt Lydia's doily was not crocheted with snow white thread, it's ivory. The crochet lace edging I selected to use for the binding was too white. It did not complement the finished quilt. I changed the color by coffee-dyeing it. While the final color is a bit unpredictable, the result is better than stark white — and Aunt Lydia was quite the coffee drinker, so there's another layer of meaning added!

Materials & Supplies

- Microwave safe glass bowl or casserole dish
- Plastic wrap
- Black, strongly-brewed coffee, to cover trim in the dish
- Kitchen colander
- 100% cotton crocheted trim

The Method

TIP 100% cotton works best as it accepts the coffee staining well. Trims of polyester or a poly/cotton blend will not accept the staining as well or with consistent results and may lose the staining if washed.

Coffee-dyed trim and the original trim.

Step 1: Place the trim to be dyed in a microwavable glass bowl or casserole dish. Pour hot coffee over the trim. Make sure that the trim is fully covered by the coffee. Stir it around to make sure all the trim is wet. Cover the bowl or casserole dish with plastic wrap or the manufacturer's cover, if you have one. If using plastic wrap, fold back a corner to vent the dish.

Step 2: Microwave for three to five minutes, depending on the wattage of your microwave. More time won't hurt. You want the trim to simmer in the coffee for a few minutes.

TIP This dye method can also be used with tea. Regular black tea, rather than an herbal tea, costs less and produces better results. Just substitute the coffee with strongly brewed tea.

Step 3: Using caution, remove from the microwave and set on a protected surface. Allow the lace and coffee to fully cool. This will take several hours. Go do something else and come back later!

Step 4: When everything has cooled down to room temperature, remove the trim and place it in the kitchen colander. Rinse under cool water until the rinse water runs clear. Straighten trim and hang to dry. Once dry, press with a hot iron with no steam.

TIP It is also possible to coffee- and tea-dye 100% cotton fabrics following these same directions — you will just need more coffee or tea and a larger pot. If the pot is too large for the microwave, bring to a boil on the stove and simmer for five to ten minutes. Make sure to stir the pot now and again to ensure good saturation. Once everything has cooled down again — taking several hours — use your washing machine's "rinse and spin" cycle and dry in the clothes dryer. Press and your fabric is ready for use.

Crochet Trim as Binding

Add interest with crochet trim binding. This process is accomplished fully by machine; no tedious hand-stitching to arrive at the finish line.

Materials & Supplies

- Flat crochet lace trim sufficient to encompass the perimeter of the quilt. (The lace used in the project is 1-1/4" wide.)
- Quilted piece ready for binding

The Method

This binding will require a bit of advance planning. With 1-1/4" trim, leave at least a 1" unquilted area around the perimeter of the quilt.

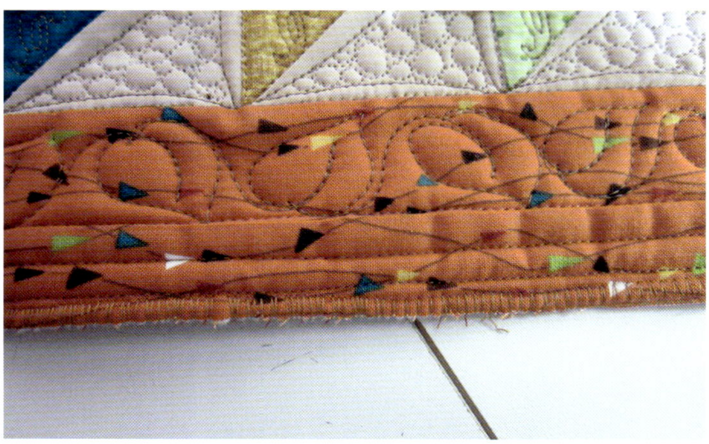

Zigzag stitch over quilt edges with matching thread.

Step 1: Prepare the quilt top. Square up the quilt top and trim edges so that there is a 1" unquilted margin around the perimeter of the quilt. If you've used lofty batting, as we did in the project sample, quilt several straight lines parallel to the edge to hold the batting down. If your batting is flatter, this quilting would not be necessary. Finish the edge with a wide, close zigzag stitch, using thread that matches the border fabric. I find that using a walking foot is beneficial for this step.

Stitch trim to the wrong side of the quilt.

Stitch small miter folds at the corners.

Turn under the raw edge of the trim before finishing the stitching.

Bring trim to quilt front, miter corners, and pin in place.

Step 2: Attach the trim. Working from the back of the quilt, stitch the trim to the edge. Make sure that the right side of the trim is facing up and that the edge of the trim is 1/4" inside the edge of the quilt. When you come to a corner, stop stitching 1/4" from the perpendicular edge. Make a small miter fold in the trim. Stitch the next side, catching the miter into your stitching. When you approach the beginning, overlap the trim by a generous inch. Fold the raw edge of the trim under and complete the stitching.

Step 3: Bring the trim to the front of the quilt. Pin in place, mitering corners.

Step 4: Stitch the trim. Set your machine for free-motion stitching and attach your preferred free motion foot. Using a thread that matches the trim, stitch around the edge of the trim. When you get to the corners, stitch the mitered fold in place by stitching down into the corner and then back up to the edge of the trim.

Using free-motion stitching, stitch the trim in place.

You have added an interesting edge finish to your quilt! The best part: It's all done by machine. If you hate hand-stitching traditional bindings, try this technique.

Chapter 9:

Aunt Anne's Poinsettias and Holly

Aunt Anne, my mother's oldest sister, kept Christmas in her heart all year long. When that time of year rolled around, her entire home was a Christmas wonderland. Everything that could hold a decoration did. Special Christmas china graced her table. No one I have ever known loved Christmas more. While we have our own Christmas traditions, I tend to favor Thanksgiving. I have crafted Christmas gifts, of course, but never made a Christmas quilt until this vintage linen piece whispered to me. "Look," it said, "don't my motifs look like wreaths? You should incorporate me into a Christmas quilt!" I did and honor my Aunt Anne.

Aunt Anne's Poinsettias and Holly, 34-3/4" x 34-3/4". Quilted by Terri Doyle.

Bead and Button Embellishments

Beads can offer just the right touch for your quilt project. The beads used in the poinsettia centers here look very much like the centers of real poinsettias. Does the thought of appliquéing dozens of tiny circles strike fear in your heart? Substitute buttons!

TIP When buying beads, you get what you pay for. I recommend frequenting your local bead shop and buying quality beads. You will find a consistency in size and color. That said, I have been very pleased with beads purchased in the larger craft stores as well. Look for beads manufactured in Japan, as they seem to be the most consistently produced.

Materials & Supplies

- Completed quilt with binding applied
- Yellow seed beads, size 8
- Green seed beads, size 11
- Beading needles size 10 or 12
- Green Nymo® beading thread, size D
- Thread Heaven® thread conditioner and protectant
- Red buttons, 3/4" and 1/2" diameter
- Red cotton thread
- Hand sewing needle

The Method – Beading

Step 1: Thread a beading needle with a length of Nymo beading thread approximately 36" long. Run the thread over the Thread Heaven to condition and strengthen the thread. Tie a knot in the end.

Make an anchoring knot in the surface of the quilt.

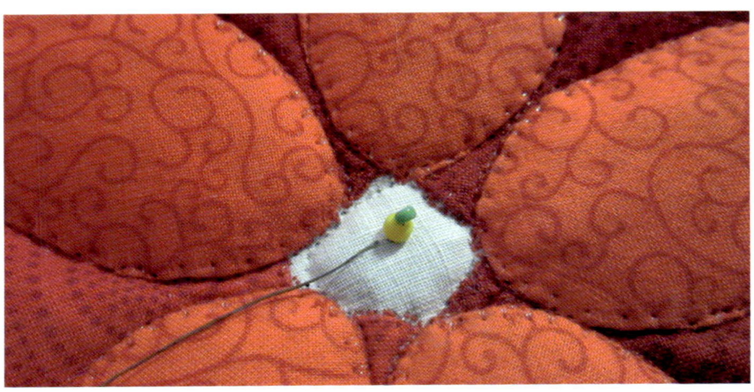

The first bead unit done.

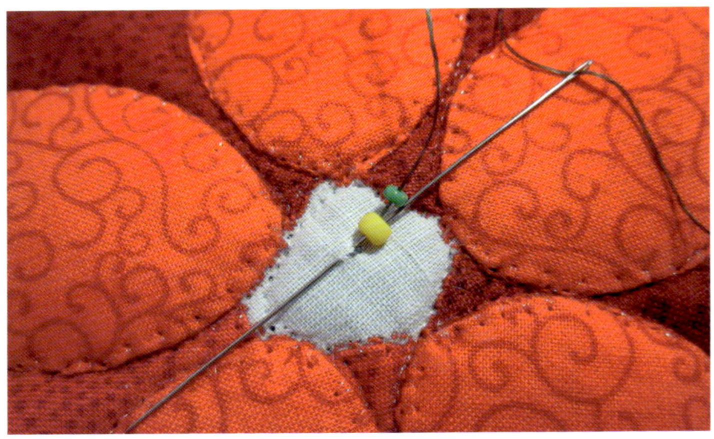

Load beads on needle and stitch to where you'll place the next unit.

Step 2: Bring the thread up from the back of the quilt to the surface near the center of the flower. Working in just the surface, make an anchoring knot. Load your needle with one yellow bead and one green bead. Stitch back through the yellow bead. Draw the needle through the top layer of the quilt to the next spot where you would like to place a bead unit. Pull the thread snuggly, but not so tightly that you wrinkle the top.

Repeat the process ...

... until the center is pleasantly filled with bead units.

Step 3: Repeat the process until the flower center is filled pleasantly with bead units. There should be no traveling stitches visible on the back of the quilt. When the last unit has been stitched, bring the needle to the back of the quilt. Knot the thread securely and finish by running in the thread about an inch. Clip the thread.

The Method – Buttons Embellishment

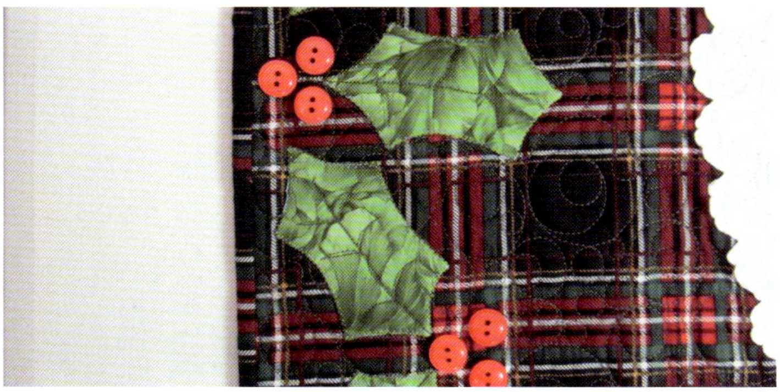

Smaller 1/2" buttons and ...

Step 1: Determine where you will place the buttons. In the sample project, I used groups of three buttons and placed the 1/2" buttons with the smaller holly leaves and the 3/4" buttons with the larger.

Tip I use doubled thread to enable me to make fewer stitches.

... larger 3/4" buttons serve as holly berries.

Strive for the appearance of neat tack stitching when attaching buttons.

TIP I prefer buttons with the holes drilled through the button for sewing rather than buttons with shanks on the back. Shank buttons stand away from the surface of the quilt and can flop over. Buttons with holes drilled through them sit flat upon the surface of the quilt. Use whatever you like...it's your quilt!

Step 2: Thread a sewing needle with the red cotton thread, double the thread, and knot the end. Bring the thread up from the back of the quilt to the top, making sure the thread passes through a hole in the button. Stab the stitch back down through the button and the quilt.

Step 3: Repeat Step 2, making five passes and striving to stitch in the same places so that the back side of the quilt looks neat. Knot the thread on the back side and run the ends in a scant inch. Clip threads and repeat for the next button.

TIP When there are four holes in a button, you have a choice in how you will attach it. Your stitches can be patterned like an "=" or like an "X". Either is fine, just be consistent!

Holly Leaf Border Pattern

Nothing says "Christmas" like holly leaves! Use these patterns to create your Christmas projects.

Materials & Supplies

- Card stock or template plastic
- Fine line Sharpie® marking pen
- Lightweight fusible interfacing
- Scraps of Christmas green fabric
- Fabric glue
- Toothpick or bamboo skewer

TIP These directions are for my preferred method of preparing and handling appliqué. Step-by-step photos appear in Chapter 2. Use the method you prefer, remembering that holly leaf templates are provided at actual size.

Pattern for smaller holly leaf. Pattern is actual size and does not include any turn under allowance.

The Method

Step 1: Create pattern templates. Trace leaf patterns on card stock or template plastic. Carefully cut out the templates.

Step 2: Trace patterns on the wrong side of lightweight fusible interfacing using the Sharpie marking pen. Reverse the orientation of the template for variety. Carefully cut on the marked lines.

Step 3: Lay the fusible leaves on the wrong side of the green fabric. Make sure that leaves are on the bias (to help with the turn under) and that there is sufficient space between leaves. Following manufacturer's instructions, fuse the leaves in place.

Step 4: Adding a 1/4" turn under allowance, cut out each leaf. Clip curved edges at 1/4" intervals. Using fabric glue and a toothpick or bamboo skewer, glue the turn under allowance to the back of the leaf.

Step 5: Place leaves on the quilt top and machine appliqué in place.

Create a holly leaf border on your next Christmas project, or create a wreath of leaves, a base for candles, or tuck them into fabric holiday floral arrangements. There are lots of possibilities!

Pattern for larger holly leaf. Pattern is actual size and does not include any turn under allowance.

Section Two: The Patterns

Chapter 10:

Naomi's Embellished Christmas Stockings

Aunt Anne's daughter, my cousin Naomi, loves Christmas just about as much as her mother. Perhaps it was something in her upbringing? After making my first Christmas-themed quilt, it begged to have companion pieces to match. We do love hanging stockings and, lacking a mantel, find that using the edge of the bookcase enables Santa to fill the stockings just as well. With a drive to continue making Christmas-themed projects, I started to hear the whisper of Christmas-themed vintage linens. "You can use us in stockings," they suggested. They were right!

Naomi's Embellished Stockings, View A (left) and View B (right), 7-1/4" wide x 18-1/2" length overall.

Embellished Christmas Stockings in Two Views

I like stockings that keep their shape. No droopy stockings for us! Follow these instructions for a stocking that keeps its shape and will hold up to years of use.

Materials & Supplies

- 3/4 yard Christmas print focus fabric for each stocking
- 1-1/2 yard lightweight fusible interfacing (I use Pellon® 931TD)
- 3/4 yard of 5/8" wide grosgrain ribbon for View A; 6" piece for View B

For View A

- 1 fat quarter fabric for band at stocking top
- Scrap of Chantilly lace with scalloped edge 7" x 16"
- 2 vintage linen coasters measuring approximately 5-1/2" in diameter

For View B

- 4 embroidered tray liners, each measuring approximately 7" x 12"
- 2 vintage linen coasters measuring approximately 4" in diameter

The Method – Cutting

Step 1: Prepare focus fabric by fusing interfacing along the lengthwise grain to the wrong side of fabric following manufacturer's instructions.

Step 2: Enlarge stocking pattern by 250% and rough cut out the pattern.

Step 3: Fold focus fabric with right sides together. Pin stocking pattern in place and cut on the cutting line.

Step 4: From the fat quarter, cut one piece measuring 5" x 16" (View A only).

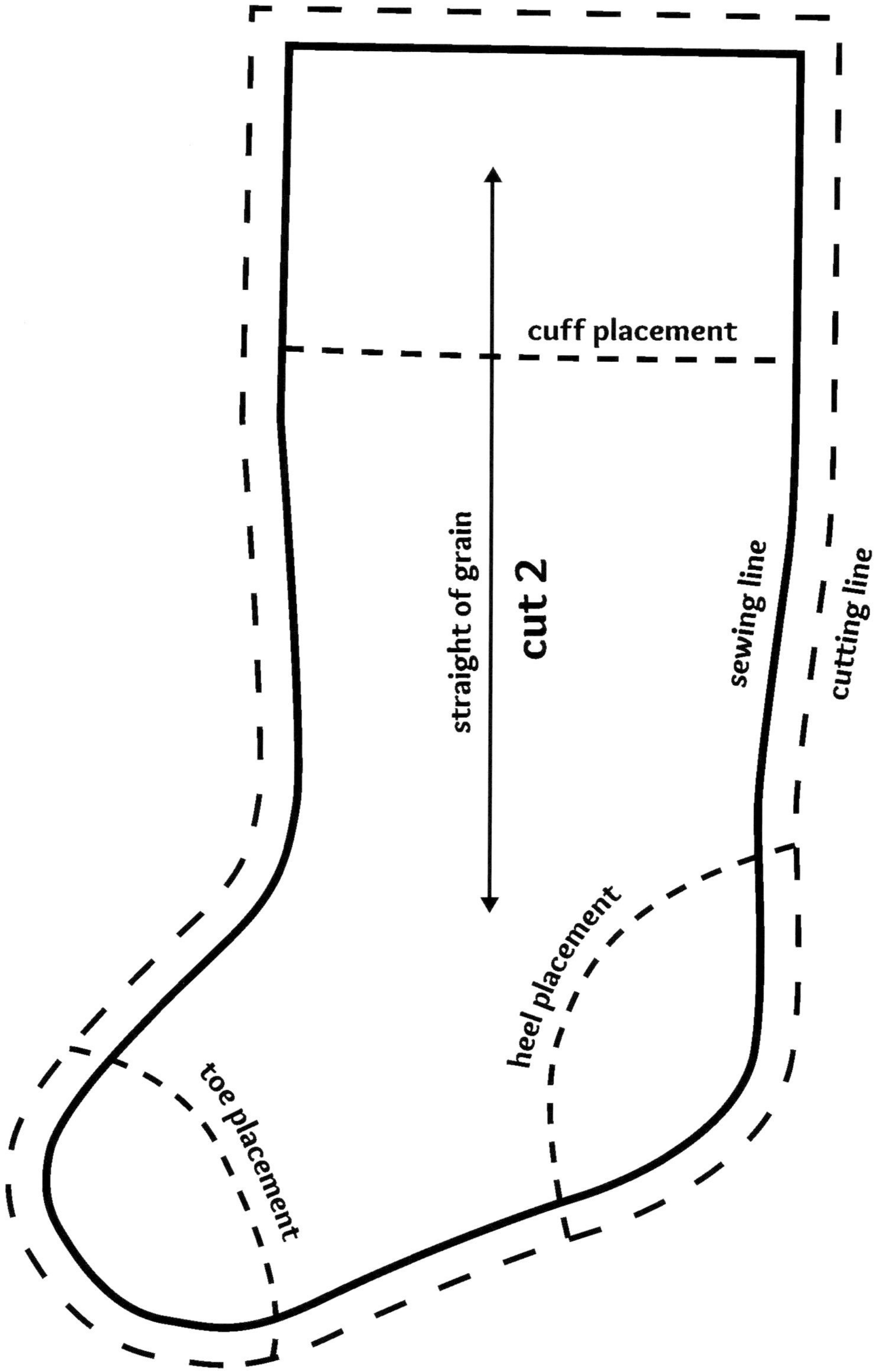

Pattern for Naomi's Embellished Christmas Stockings. Copy at 250% for full size pattern.

The Method – Assembling

View A embellished and trimmed.

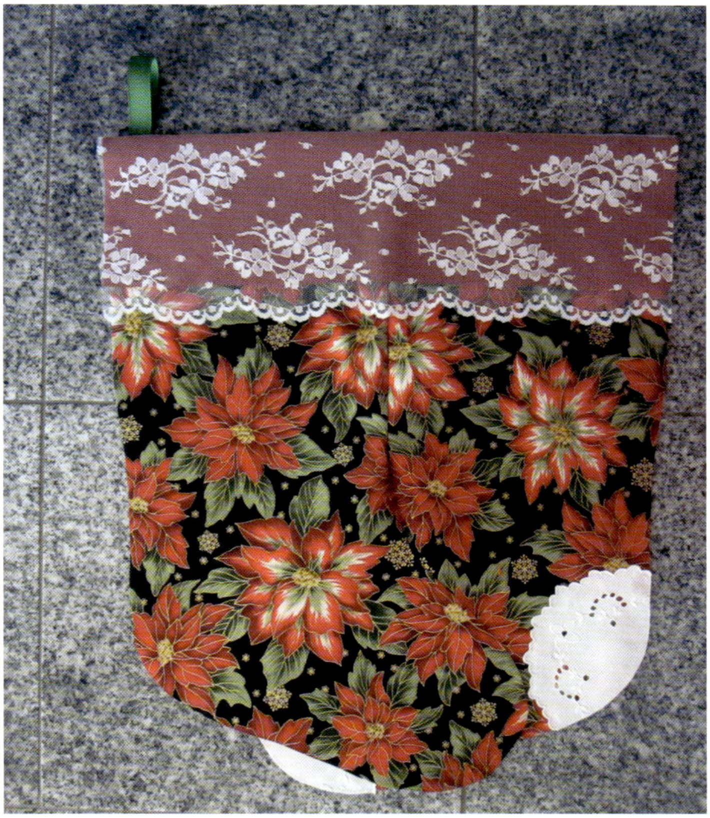

View A with top band stitched in place.

Band is finished with green ribbon trim.

Step 1: Embellish the right side of one stocking piece. For View A, place one 5-1/2" doily to represent the stocking toe and one 5-1/2" doily to represent the heel. Appliqué in place and cut the excess away at the edge of the stocking. For View B, place one 4" doily in the toe area and one 4" doily in the heel area, taking care that the doilies are within the seam allowance.

Step 2: With right sides together and using a 1/2" seam allowance, stitch the side seam of the toe edge for about 7". Press the seam open.

Step 3: Make the hanging loop. Cut a 6" piece of 5/8" grosgrain ribbon. Bring the raw edges of the ribbon together, creating the hanging loop. On the wrong side of the back stocking piece, with all raw edges even, pin the loop 3/4" from the side edge of the stocking. Baste in place and remove the pin.

Assembling band for View B.

View B with band stitched in place.

Step 4: Attaching the stocking band. For View A, layer the Chantilly lace over the right side of the fabric band. Have the raw edge of the band at the base of the lace scallops. Pin the right side of the band to the wrong side of the stocking and stitch with a 1/2" seam. Turn the top to the right side of the stocking and press. Lay the remaining grosgrain ribbon over the raw edges of the top band. Stitch on both sides of the ribbon, covering the raw edge of the band, leaving the scallops of the lace showing. For View B, overlap the vintage linen pieces, ensuring that they measure 16" across. Pin and baste in place. Remove pins and trim to 6". Pin the right side of the top doily assembly to the wrong side of the stocking. Stitch with a 1/2" seam. Turn to the right side of stocking and press.

View A completed and ready for Santa's visit!

Step 5: Complete the stocking. With right sides together, stitch around the remainder of the stocking using a 1/2" seam allowance. Clip the seam allowance every 1/4" to 1/2", especially in the curves. Turn the stocking to the right side, smoothing the seam with your fingers. Open the seam next to the hanging loop. Top stitch close to the edge to keep the seam open. Press well. Hang your stocking and await a visit from Santa!

Chapter 11:

GG Says, "Shhhh . . . Baby's Sleeping!"

My mother, Bernice, was very good about not pressuring me to make her a grandmother. When I finally announced the news, at age 29, her response was, "Oh! Thank goodness; I thought it would never happen for me." Collectively, we have not been so kind to my daughters, nagging them unmercifully to offer Bernice Great-Grandmother status and allow me to be a Grandmother. While we recognize the decision is not about us and we try to wait patiently for my daughters' lives to unfold, that does not prevent us from preparing. We have started a GG and G'ma Hope Chest. This charming vintage dresser piece whispered that it would like to be included there.

Shhh...Baby's Sleeping, approximately 12-1/2" x 7"

Shhhh...Baby's Sleeping Door Hanger Pillow Pattern

How I wish I had one of these when my girls were babies. Hanging this pillow on the doorknob during nap time puts the household on alert not to disturb Baby's slumber.

Materials & Supplies

- 1/2 yard baby print fabric
- Thin cotton batting – 17" x 11-1/2"
- 1-1/3 yard 1-1/2" wide wired ribbon
- 1-1/4 yard pre-gathered lace 1-1/4" wide
- Vintage tray liner doily measuring approx. 11" x 5-1/2"

The Method – Cutting

Step 1: Cut baby print fabric into 4 pieces: For pillow top, one 15" x 9-1/2" piece and one 17" x 11-1/2"; for pillow envelope backing, two 8-1/4" x 17".

NOTE All cutting instructions assume a doily of 11" x 5-1/2". If your doily's measurements are different, adjust these cutting and assembly directions accordingly.

The Method – Assembly

Step 1: Prepare doily. Transfer "Shhhh....." to the center of the doily, using your preferred method. Chapter 5 offers a number of suggestions. In the sample project, the letters are painted using Jacquard™ Textile Color.

Prepare doily and center on background fabric.

Step 2: Make the pillow top. Center the doily on one of the 15" x 9-1/2" pieces of background fabric and appliqué in place. Here, I stitched close to the edge of the doily using the free-motion capabilities of my machine. Layer the top, batting, and backing (17" x 11-1/2" print fabric). Quilt as desired. Trim quilted piece to 13-1/2" x 8-1/4".

TIP You can buy custom-made pillow inserts quite reasonably. This means that you have no size restrictions in the pillows you create and can design freely to your materials, instead of trying to design to a size pillow found in stores. I have had great luck with PillowsXpress™ (www.pillowsxpress.com). You choose from various stuffing options and, of course, specify the size of your pillow. The web site offers hints on how to order the size that will provide you just the look you want for your project. Save on shipping costs by ordering multiple pillow inserts. Search "custom pillow forms" on the Internet for additional suppliers.

Add lace trim and wired ribbon for hanging.

Step 3: Add lace and ribbon trims. Fold under 1/2" on gathered lace trim. Beginning at the center bottom of the pillow top, pin in place, around the edge, mitering trim for fullness in the corners. Machine baste in place close to the raw edge. Cut two 24" pieces of wire-edged ribbon. Baste each piece on the top edge of the pillow top 2-1/2" in from the side edges.

Step 4: Prepare pillow backing assembly. With wrong sides together, fold each backing piece in half to create two backing pieces measuring 8-1/4" x 8-1/2". Top stitch both pieces along the folds. Overlap backing pieces so that the layered pieces measure 8-1/4" x 13-1/2". Machine baste, overlapping sections close to the edges to hold the backing in place.

Step 5: Assemble the pillow. Layer the pillow backing assembly on the prepared top. Stitch around the entire outer edge of the pillow with a 1/4" seam. Turn the pillow to right side through the overlap opening in the pillow backing. Press well. Insert pillow form. Tie the wire ribbon into a bow. Hang on the doorknob and help Baby enjoy restful sleep.

Chapter 12:

Tracy and Caitlyn's Tooth Fairy Pillow

I understand why the legend of the Tooth Fairy was created. How scary to have one's teeth come out! Visits from the Tooth Fairy, with the little gifts she leaves behind, help ease this transition for children. My daughters, Tracy and Caitlyn, both had tooth fairy pillows when they were of the age when teeth were being lost. My daughters and I were shopping in a huge vintage store when I spotted this tiny crocheted doily. It whispered, "I have a ring of blossoms where the fairies dance. I should be used as the pocket on a tooth fairy pillow." Of course, I listened to the doily and this tooth fairy pillow is destined for the GG and G'ma Hope Chest!

Tooth Fairy Pillow, approximately 11" x 8"

Tooth Fairy Pillow

Make the Tooth Fairy's job easier. The lost tooth goes in the pocket. When the Tooth Fairy visits, she replaces the tooth with her gift. Much easier than rooting around under pillows and in tangled sheets!

About the Poem

The poem used in this project is an originally-written haiku. Permission is granted for you to use it for personal use. If the poem isn't to your liking, search on the internet for "tooth fairy poems." Lots of options will present themselves, but please be sure that you honor the writer's copyright. Here is the haiku used in the sample project:

Tooth Fairy, Dearest,
Trade me for my tooth that's here.
Thanks for your visit!

Materials & Supplies

- Fat quarter of fabric with printed tooth fairy poem (see tip)
- Fat quarter coordinating fabric for backing
- Scrap of fabric for doily lining
- Thin cotton batting, 14" x 11" scrap
- Vintage doily measuring approximately 4" in diameter
- Variety of floral embellishments, project used purchased ribbon flowers, leaves peeled from ivy silk plant, and seed beads.
- Fairy embellishment: For the project, the fairy was painted and appliquéd. You might find commercial printed fabric with fairies or an embroidery module to achieve similar results

NOTE Depending on the layout of your poem, for the fairy embellishment, as well as your vintage doily, adjustment in materials and/or cutting may be necessary. Instructions given here are based on the sample project.

The Method – Cutting

NOTE Plan the placement of your embellishments and cut your project as needed. Instructions here are based on the sample project.

Cut printed fabric to 13" x 10". From coordinating fat quarter, cut one 15" x 12" (for pillow top backing) and two 8-3/4" x 16" (for pillow backing)

TIP It is possible to order custom printed fabric with just about anything printed on it. Wanting a delicate look to my letters, I chose this method. The poem in the sample project is an originally-written haiku. I selected the font, color, and layout and created a file that was uploaded to the fabric printer. I ordered white Kona® cotton in the fat quarter size. Then, I just waited for my order to arrive. You'll find custom printed fabric companies on the Resources List page.

The Method – Assembling

Step 1: Prepare doily. Line the doily. For the project, a circle of fabric was cut, edges turned under, and that was appliquéd to the back of the doily. This helps maintain the shape and covers any openings in the doily.

Line the doily to help maintain its shape and cover any openings.

Appliqué the fairy embellishment to the poem-printed fabric.

Step 2: Make pillow top. Embellish the poem-printed fabric with the fairy. In the sample project, the fairy is fused to the surface and a tiny blanket stitch was used all around the outer edge of the appliqué. Layer the pillow top backing, batting, and top and quilt as desired. The sample project is lightly quilted with feathered elements representing fronds. Embellish with leaves, flowers, and beads. Ensure that all embellishments are firmly attached. Mine are all firmly hand sewn down. Add the lined doily. Make sure to leave an opening at the top to insert the tooth and then leave the fairy gift. A few reinforcing stitches at the openings are recommended. Trim the completed top to 11-1/4" x 8-3/4".

Layer the pillow top and add quilting.

Embellish with silk leaves and flowers, making sure all are firmly sewn.

Step 3: Prepare pillow backing assembly. With wrong sides together, fold each pillow envelope backing piece in half to create two backing pieces measuring 8-3/4" x 8". Top stitch both pieces along the folds. Overlap backing pieces so that the layered piece measures 11-1/4" x 8-3/4". Machine baste, overlapping sections, close to the edges to hold backing in place.

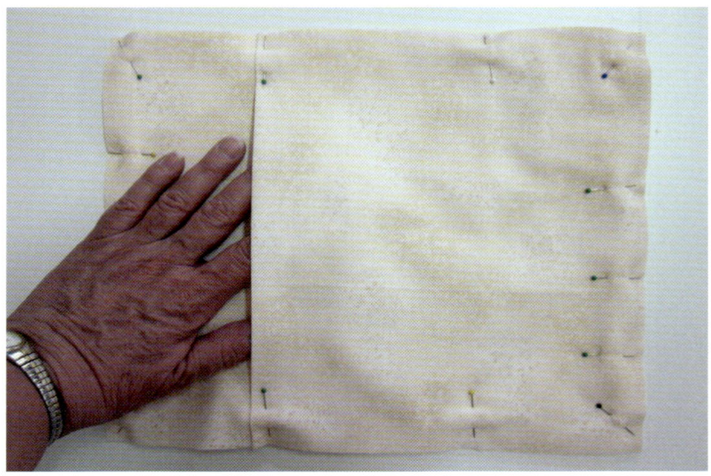

Layer the pillow backing over the prepared top, stitch, and turn to complete the pillow.

Step 4: Assemble the pillow. Layer the pillow backing assembly on the prepared top. Stitch around the entire outer edge of the pillow with a 1/4" seam. Clip corners to reduce bulk. Turn pillow to right side through the overlap opening in the pillow backing. Press well. Insert pillow form.

Await the loss of a tooth — and a visit from the Tooth Fairy!

Chapter 13:

Bill's Maple Leaf Rag Table Runner

Thanksgiving was my late husband's favorite holiday. The meal was so important to him that, in our first year together, he asked me to prepare it in October just to be sure he would be satisfied on the actual holiday. Although I thought the request quite daft, I did it anyway and we enjoyed two Thanksgivings that year.

The Maple Leaf block has always been a favorite and speaks of the Midwest Autumn colors I miss as a desert dweller. When I saw this single leaf-shaped doily edged in the colors of autumn, it whispered to me, "I would complement the Maple Leaf block, don't you think?" I believe so!

Maple Leaf Rag Table Runner, 16-3/4" x 41-3/4"

Maple Leaf Rag Table Runner

Imagine this table runner gracing your table throughout the Fall. If a leaf-shaped doily is hard to find, just substitute a fourth Maple Leaf block and your project is complete!

Materials & Supplies

- Leaf-shaped doily measuring approximately 6-1/2" x 6-1/2"
- Scrap of cream-colored fabric to back leaf approximately 8" x 8"
- 1/2 yard cream for maple leaf blocks and block sashing
- Scraps of various values of reds/rusts for maple leaves
- Fat Quarter of gold/cream check for inner border
- 1/2 yard leaf print for outer border and binding
- Thin cotton batting, piece to measure 46" x 20"
- Backing fabric measuring 50" x 24"
- Clover® Bias Tape Maker (6mm – 1/4" size)

The Method – Cutting

Each leaf uses four values of red/rust for leaves and cream for the background.

Step 1: For each leaf, cut:

- Cream: Six 2" x 2" squares; two 2" x 3-1/2" rectangles; one 3-1/2" x 3-1/2" square; and two 2-1/2" x 4-1/2" rectangle
- Color A (leaf tip): One 3" x 5" rectangle
- Color B (two leaf sections): Two 2" x 3-1/2" rectangles
- Color C (leaf center and two leaf sections): One 2" x 2" square; two 2" x 3-1/2" rectangle
- Color D (leaf stem and two leaf sections): One 4" x 4" square; two 2" x 3-1/2" rectangles

Step 2: Leaf Doily Background: One 8" x 8" square

Step 3: Cream Maple Leaf Block Background: Three 1-1/2" x 7-3/4" for block sashing

Step 4: Cream/Gold Check: Five 2" x 22" strips

Step 5: Leaf Print: Three 3-1/2" strips by width of fabric for borders and three 2-1/2" strips by width of fabric for binding

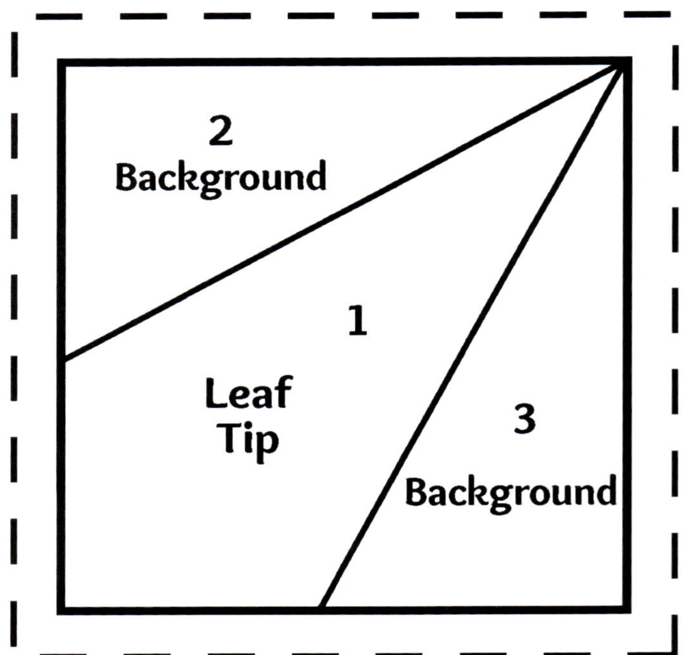

Foundation piecing pattern for Maple Leaf block tip.

NOTE Cutting instructions for the outer border/leaf print assumes 42" width of usable fabric. If your selection is narrower, adjust yardage and cutting instructions to accommodate.

The Method – Assembly

Step 1: Prepare doily block. Center the leaf doily on the selected background fabric. Appliqué using your preferred method. Trim background to 7-3/4" x 7-3/4".

Step 2: Make three Maple Leaf blocks. For each block:

a. Copy the paper piecing pattern for the leaf tip. For each leaf, paper piece one 3" x 5" leaf tip with two 2-1/2" x 4-1/2" background pieces. Piece in numerical order. Trim seam allowances around outside of block to 1/4". Unfinished block should measure 3-1/2" x 3-1/2".

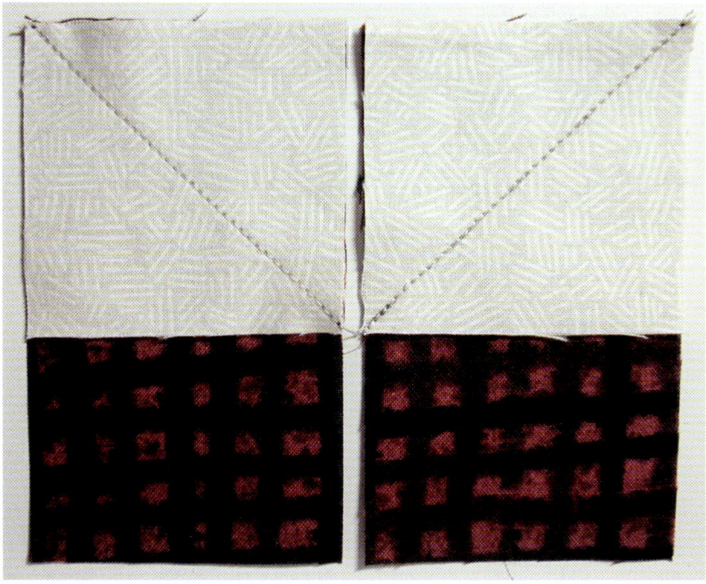

Make three sets of leaf tips, taking care that the diagonal seams run in opposite directions.

b. Draw a diagonal line on the wrong side of six 2" x 2" cream background squares. With right sides together, layer against the six 2" x 3-1/2" leaf section colors. Refer to the photograph for the orientation of the tip angles. You'll have three sets of leaf tips, each measuring 2" x 3-1/2".

c. To make the leaf stem, from the 4" x 4" stem piece, cut a diagonal 1" bias strip from the center of the piece. Using a Clover Bias Tape Maker (6mm – 1/4" size) and following the manufacturer's instructions, create bias tape. Curving the bias tape and tucking in the raw edge, appliqué the stem onto the 3-1/2" x 3-1/2" background square.

The nine units that create the Maple Leaf block.

Piece the units into three rows.

Assemble the rows into the finished block.

d. Following the photograph, layout the leaf block and stitch together. Blocks will measure 7-3/4" x 7-3/4" (unfinished). Make three Maple Leaf blocks.

Step 3: Assemble the center section of the runner. Layout the Maple Leaf blocks and doily leaf block in a manner pleasing to you. I rotated the position of the leaf stems to make it appear as if the leaves were dancing on the wind. Stitch a 1-1/2" x 7-3/4" sashing strip between each block. Press seams toward the sashing strips.

Step 4: Add inner border. Cut two pieces of the cream/gold check at 2" x 7-3/4". Sew one piece to either end of the runner center. Press seam toward inner border. Measure the length of your center section, including inner borders just added. Seam remaining inner border strips end to end and cut two pieces this measurement. Sew to either side of runner. Press seam toward inner border.

Step 5: Add the outer border. Measure the width of the runner. Cut two outer border sections this measurement and sew to the ends of runner. Press seams toward outer border. Sew remaining width of fabric strips to length of runner. Press seams to outer border.

Step 6: Layer, quilt as desired, and bind. Enjoy a festive fall table!

Chapter 14:

Leslie's Personalized Journal

Leslie and I first met when she was a student in one of my grant writing seminars. Fast forward to several years later. We reconnected when I transitioned a client to her. Finding we had much in common, we became good friends. Leslie is a beader and has gifted me with several lovely pieces. I developed this journal pattern and gifted Leslie with one. She cried when she opened the package, a sure sign that the gift is liked, and she uses it for all her meeting notes. There is nothing better than knowing your gift is not only appreciated, but useful. Vintage linen coasters are small and whisper in tiny voices, "I'd make a lovely monogram in almost any project!"

Personalized Journals, approximately 8" x 10" when closed.

Personalized Journal

The notebooks used to create this personalized journal are readily available and inexpensive. I buy mine at my grocery store where they are usually priced at less than $1.00 and often much less during "Back to School" season. Once the current notebook is filled, just insert a new one. With a vintage linen coaster and some beautiful fabrics and ribbon, you can create an impressive, personalized gift!

Materials & Supplies

- Top Flight Composition Book, 100 sheets (200 pages), measuring 9.75" x 7.5"
- Vintage doily coaster, approximately 5-1/2" in diameter
- 3/4 yard focus fabric
- Fat quarter accent fabric
- 1 yard Medium weight fusible interfacing
- Fusible fleece or thin batting 13" x 17-1/4"
- 1-1/4"yards 5/8" wide ribbon
- Ballpoint pen with pocket clip

The Method – Cutting

Step 1: From the Focus Fabric: Cut two at 13-3/4" x 18" for outside of cover; one at 10-3/4" x 16-1/8" for cover lining; and two at 10-3/4" x 13" for pockets holding composition book

Step 2: From the Fusible Fleece: Cut one at 13-3/4" x 18"

Step 3: From the Accent Fabric: Cut one at 10-3/4" x 2-1/2" for spine; two at 4-1/2" x 2-1/2" for pen holder; and one at 4-1/2" x 4-1/4" for business card holder (optional)

Step 4: From the Medium-weight Fusible Interfacing: Cut two at 10-1/4" x 6-1/2" for pockets holding composition book; one at 10-1/4" x 15-5/8"; one at 10-3/4" x 2" for spine; and one at 4" x 2" for pen holder

The Method – Assembling

Step 1: Prepare the doily. Using your preferred method, monogram the doily. For hints and tips, see Chapter Five.

Place monogrammed doily and ribbons and secure with stitching.

Layer and quilt the cover and trim to size.

Step 2: Prepare the outside of the cover. Locate the horizontal and vertical centers of one 13-3/4" x 18" focus fabric. Mark with pins along fabric edges. Cut 5/8" ribbon into an 18" piece and a 24" piece. Center the monogrammed doily in the center of the right half of the fabric piece. Assuming a 5-1/2" doily, that would be approximately 1-1/4" right of the center line and 4" down from the top. Pin doily in place. Slip 1/2" of the 18" piece of ribbon under the center of the right hand side of the doily. Pin in place. Slip 1/2" of the 24" piece of ribbon under the center of the left hand side of the doily. Pin in place. Appliqué doily in place using your favorite method and catching in the ends of the ribbons. Following manufacturer's directions, fuse the fusible fleece to the wrong side of the cover. Layer with the other 13-3/4" x 18" piece of focus fabric and quilt as desired. Trim quilted piece to 10-3/4" x 16-1/8".

Step 3: Prepare the center spine and pen holder. To prepare the center spine, fuse 10-3/4" x 2" interfacing to wrong side of 10-3/4" x 2-1/2" accent fabric, centering the interfacing on the accent fabric. Press under 1/4" on both long ends of the spine. To prepare the pen holder, fuse the 4" x 2" interfacing to the wrong side of one of the 4-1/2" x 2-1/2" pieces of accent fabric, centering the interfacing on the back of the piece. With right sides together and using a 1/4" seam, stitch the top and bottom. Turn to the right side and press well. The side with the interfacing is the "right" side of the piece. Top stitch both edges. Fold in half lengthwise and press lightly.

Attach the center spine and pen holder.

Step 4: Attach the center spine and pen holder. Matching the center of the cover and the center of the spine, pin the spine in place. Make sure that the left ribbon is under the spine. On the right side, slip 1/4" of the pen holder under the edge of the spine and re-pin. Stitch close to both edges of the spine, catching in the pen holder. Reinforce by stitching both edges a second time. The outside cover is complete!

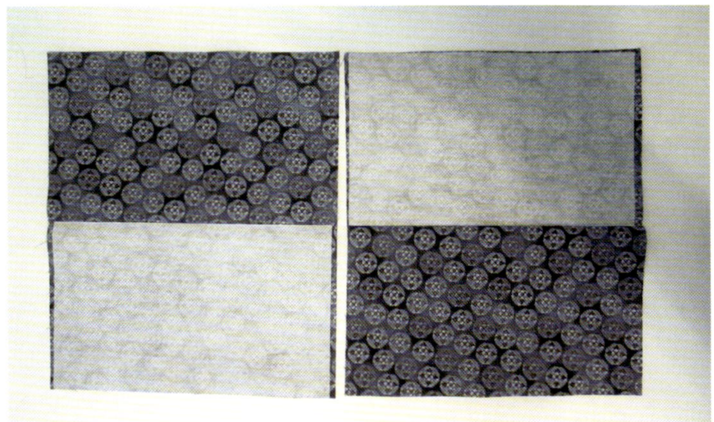

Prepare the cover pockets with fusible interfacing.

Step 5: Prepare cover pockets. Press the two pieces of focus fabric measuring 10-3/4" x 13" in half (resulting in two pieces measuring 10-3/4" x 6-1/2"). Fuse one 10-1/4" x 6-1/2" piece of interfacing to the left side of one and to the right side of the other. The fused side will become the right side of the pocket. Press again along the fold and top stitch along the folded edge.

Step 6 (Optional): Prepare and attach the business card holder. Fold the 4-1/2" x 4-1/4" piece of accent fabric right sides together, folding along the slightly longer side. Leaving a small opening for turning at the longer edge, stitch around each side with a 1/4" seam. Turn to the right side and press well. Top stitch along the folded edge. Center on the lower portion of the left hand pocket and stitch in place close to the edges, leaving the top edge free. Reinforce top edges.

Inside cover with business card holder on the left pocket.

Step 7: Complete the inside cover. Fuse the 10-1/4" x 15-5/8" piece of fusible interfacing to the wrong side of the 10-3/4" x 16-1/8" piece of focus fabric, leaving allowances on all sides. Pin the left and right pockets in place. Machine baste 1/8" from raw edges.

Completed cover – outside.

Insert composition book.

Tie a bow, add a pen, and enjoy!

Step 8: Assemble the cover. With the right sides facing, layer the outside and inside pieces. Stitch each side, leaving an opening on the left hand side for turning. Take care to make sure the ribbons are not caught into the sewing. Clip corners. Turn to the right side and steam press well. Make sure that you press 1/4" in at the turning opening. Pin the ribbons into place at the edges of the cover. Top stitch close to the edge around the entire cover, catching in ribbons and closing the turning opening. Notch the ends of the ribbon to prevent fraying. Insert the composition book by sliding the front and back covers into the pockets of the quilted cover. Tie ribbon ends into a bow. Insert the pen in the pen holder and your business card in the inside pocket.

Chapter 15:

Dad Thinks, "It's a Grand Old Flag"

My dad was an enlisted man in the U.S. Army when Pearl Harbor was attacked. He served over five years and throughout the duration of World War II. He never talked about his experiences. He died of a massive heart attack at age fifty-four; I was sixteen years old. It wasn't until I read, as an adult, Tom Brokaw's *The Greatest Generation* that I understood more about this part of my father's life. I wish we could have had an adult relationship. I miss him every day.

How lucky I was to have this red doily whisper to me. While shopping in a charming antique shop, a lovely pair of vintage white gloves whispered to me as well. "Use me in a quilt," they suggested. "Pair me with that lovely red doily and create something to honor your father's service." Daddy, this one is for you.

It's a Grand Old Flag, 20" x 20"

It's a Grand Old Flag

Perfect to display on the 4th of July, Memorial Day, and Veterans Day, this quilt celebrates America and all the good she stands for.

Materials & Supplies

- American Flag on "pole" measuring 4" x 6" (see Resource List)
- 1 gold tassel, commercially purchased trim
- Vintage red doily, approximately 8" in diameter
- Vintage left hand white glove
- 13-1/2" x 13-1/2" navy blue star print fabric (center background)
- 1/2 yard red for stripes and binding
- Fat quarter of white for stripes
- Scrap of navy to yield four 4" x 4" squares for cornerstones
- Scraps of white with silver sparkles for stars (need 9" x 9" piece)
- Fusible web (9" x 9" piece)
- Batting measuring 24" x 24"
- Backing fabric measuring 24" x 24"

The Method – Cutting

Step 1: From the Red Fabric: Cut in half to create 2 fat quarters – from one fat quarter, cut seven 1-1/2" x 22" strips; from remaining fabric, cut five 2-1/2" x 22" strips for binding.

Step 2: From the White Fat Quarter: Cut six 1-1/2" x 22" strips.

Step 3: From the Navy: Cut four 4" x 4" squares for cornerstones.

The Method – Assembly

Step 1: Prepare the striped outer border. The outer border mimics the stripes in the American flag. Beginning and ending with red, stitch alternating red and white strips together. Press seams toward red, taking care to keep seams straight. Finished strip set should be 13-1/2" wide. Cut into four border segments, each at 4" wide.

Step 2: Prepare the cornerstones. Trace four stars on to the fusible web. Following manufacturer's instructions, fuse to the wrong side of the white/silver fabric. Cut out the stars. Again, following manufacturer's instructions, fuse the stars to the 4" x 4" navy squares. Note the orientation of the stars in the project photo, one point is straight up at the center top, which ensures a good fit of the fused appliqué.

Tip To prevent the navy from shadowing through your white stars, cut out the center of the fusible web, leaving about 1/4" around the outside, before fusing to the white/silver.

Step 3: Complete border preparations. Sew the star cornerstones to the right and left side of two red/white striped border segments, taking care with the orientation of the stars. Press seam toward stars. These will become the top and bottom borders.

Step 4: Prepare center section. Matching the center of the red doily and the center of the 13-1/2" x 13-1/2" navy star print, pin and appliqué the doily in place. I stitched mine by machine around the edge of the linen and hand stitched the tatted edging in place.

Step 5: Add borders. Using 1/4" seams throughout, sew a red/white stripe border segment to the left and right sides of the center square. Press seam toward the center square. Nesting the corner stone seams and taking care with the orientation of the stars, sew top and bottom border segments. Press seam toward center block.

Step 6: Layer and quilt. Layer the backing, batting, and quilt top and quilt as desired. Matching thread color to the fabric, I quilted pebbles in the center of the doily and the background of the border cornerstones; a cross-hatch grid in the navy/star print; free-motion "waves" in each red and white stripe; and with silver metallic thread, a star over each of the four cornerstone stars.

Arrange and pin the glove in place, testing the placement of the flag.

Pull back the top of the glove and stitch the channel pocket.

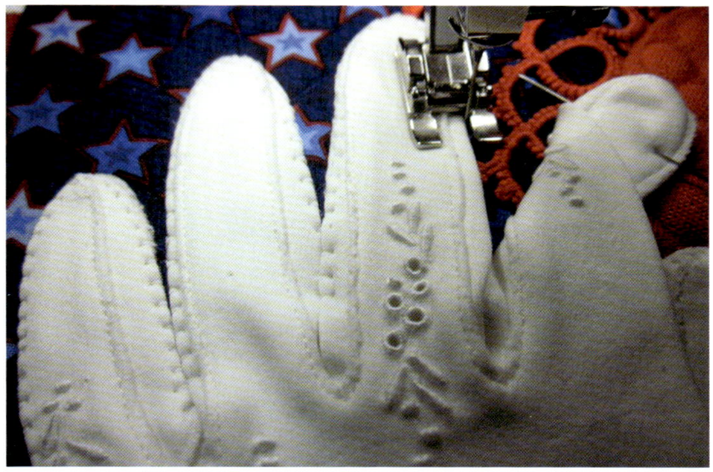

Machine appliqué the glove in place, leaving the channel open for the flag.

Step 7: Appliqué white glove. Shape the white glove to look like a hand is holding the flag. Pin in place on the quilt surface and test the placement of the flag. You will need to create a channel pocket to hold the pole. Pull back the top of the glove and pin a channel where the flag pole rests. Stitch the channel on the inside of the glove through the entire quilt top. Machine appliqué around the edge of the white glove, making sure to leave an opening where the flag will slide into the channel.

Step 8: Bind the edges of the quilt.

Step 9: Add the flag and finish. Slide the pole into the channel. Machine appliqué the flag to the surface of the quilt. I only stitched on the top and bottom of the flag because I wanted it to have a looser/freer look. You might choose more stitching. Use a slip knot to attach the tassel at the top of the flag pole. I added a drop of clear-drying glue to keep it in place. Add a label and hanging sleeve and enjoy your quilt!

Resource List

Where to Buy

Doilies:

eBay – www.ebay.com
etsy – www.etsy.com

Preferred Fabric Paints:

Jacquard® Textile Colors:
Dharma Trading Company – www.dharmatrading.com
Dick Blick Art Materials – www.dickblick.com
Perfect Pigment™ Acrylic Paint:
USArtQuest – www.usartquest.com

Custom Pillow Inserts:

PillowsXpress™ – www.pillowsxpress.com

Custom Printed Fabric:

Spoonflower – www.spoonflower.com
Fabric on Demand – www.fabricondemand.com

American Flags:

American Flags 4 Less – www.americanflags4less.com

Transfer Artists Paper:

C&T Publishing – www.ctpub.com

RetroClean Textile Cleaning Product:

Retro Clean – www.retroclean.com